THINGS SCIENTISTS DON'T KNOW YET

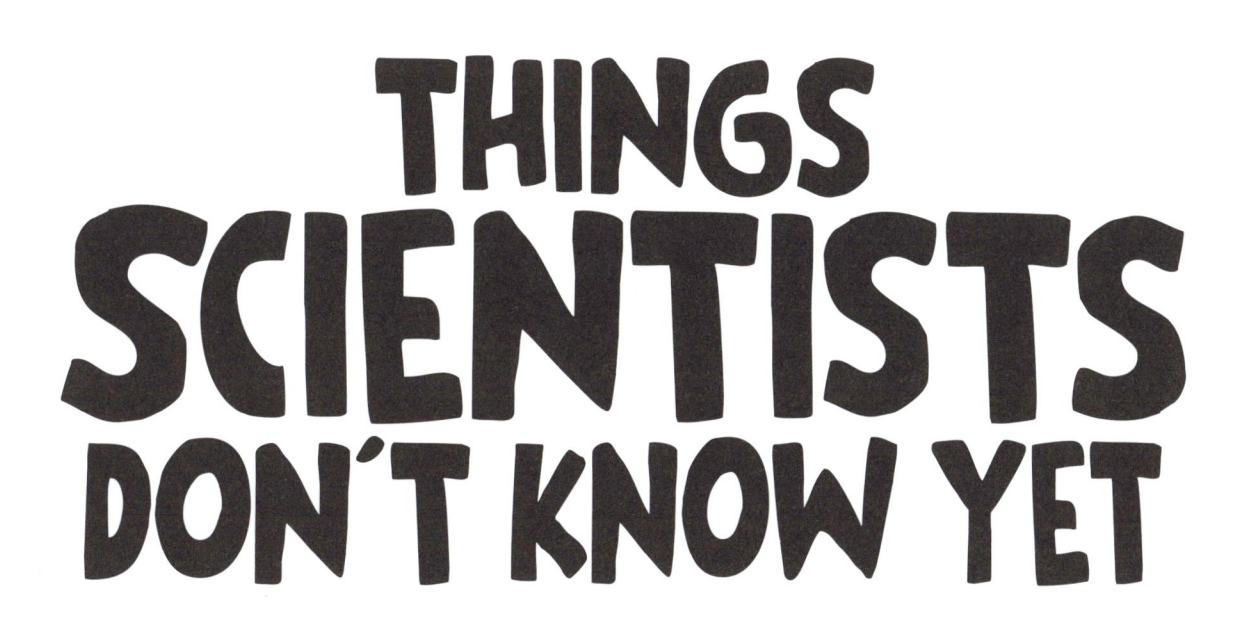

DK Penguin Random House

Author Peter Gallivan
Illustrator Daniela Gamba
Consultant Dr Kat Day

Project Editor Edward Pearce
Senior Editor Jenny Sich
US Senior Editor Shannon Beatty
Senior Art Editor Rachael Grady
Managing Editor Francesca Baines
Managing Art Editor Philip Letsu
Senior Picture Researcher Sakshi Saluja
Rights and Permissions Specialist Priya Singh
Production Editor Gillian Reid
Production Controller Ena Matagic
Publisher James Mitchem
Art Director Mabel Chan

First American Edition, 2025
Published in the United States by DK Publishing,
a division of Penguin Random House LLC
1745 Broadway, 20th Floor, New York, NY 10019

Text copyright © The Royal Institution 2025
Copyright in the layouts, design, and all other elements of the Work
(including, for the avoidance of doubt, all artwork not supplied by
the Proprietor) shall be vested in the Publishers.

Copyright © 2025 Dorling Kindersley Limited
25 26 27 28 29 10 9 8 7 6 5 4 3 2 1
001–342118–Nov/2025

All rights reserved.
No part of this publication may be reproduced, stored in or introduced
into a retrieval system, or transmitted, in any form, or by any means
(electronic, mechanical, photocopying, recording, or otherwise),
without the prior written permission of the copyright owner.
No part of this publication may be used or reproduced in any manner for
the purpose of training artificial intelligence technologies or systems.

Published in Great Britain by Dorling Kindersley Limited,
in association with the Royal Institution of Great Britain.
Registered charity no. 227938

ISBN: 978-0-5939-6536-8

DK books are available at special discounts when purchased
in bulk for sales promotions, premiums, fund-raising,
or educational use.
For details, contact: DK Publishing Special Markets,
1745 Broadway, 20th Floor, New York, NY 10019
SpecialSales@dk.com

Printed and bound in China

www.dk.com

MIX
Paper | Supporting
responsible forestry
FSC® C018179

This book was made with Forest
Stewardship Council™ certified
paper – one small step in DK's
commitment to a sustainable future.
Learn more at www.dk.com/uk/
information/sustainability

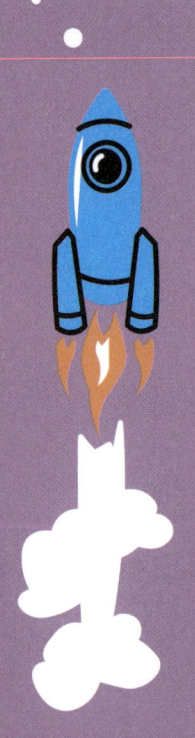

THINGS SCIENTISTS DON'T KNOW YET

WRITTEN BY
PETER GALLIVAN

ILLUSTRATED BY
DANIELA GAMBA

CONTENTS

- A world of scientists — 6
- Hunting for facts — 8
- Why are there so many beetles? — 10
- Why did the woolly mammoth go extinct? — 12
- How do monarch butterflies find their way? — 14
- Why did the Stegosaurus have plates? — 16
- Why do things keep evolving into crabs? — 18
- Why do animals need sleep? — 20
- How did life begin? — 22
- How many species are there on Earth? — 24
- What is in the depths of the ocean? — 26
- Where did all the water on Earth come from? — 28
- Will we ever be able to predict earthquakes? — 30
- How do plants communicate with each other? — 32
- Why did flowers take over the world? — 34
- How do sunflowers follow the sun? — 36
- How will the universe end? — 38
- Do aliens exist? — 40

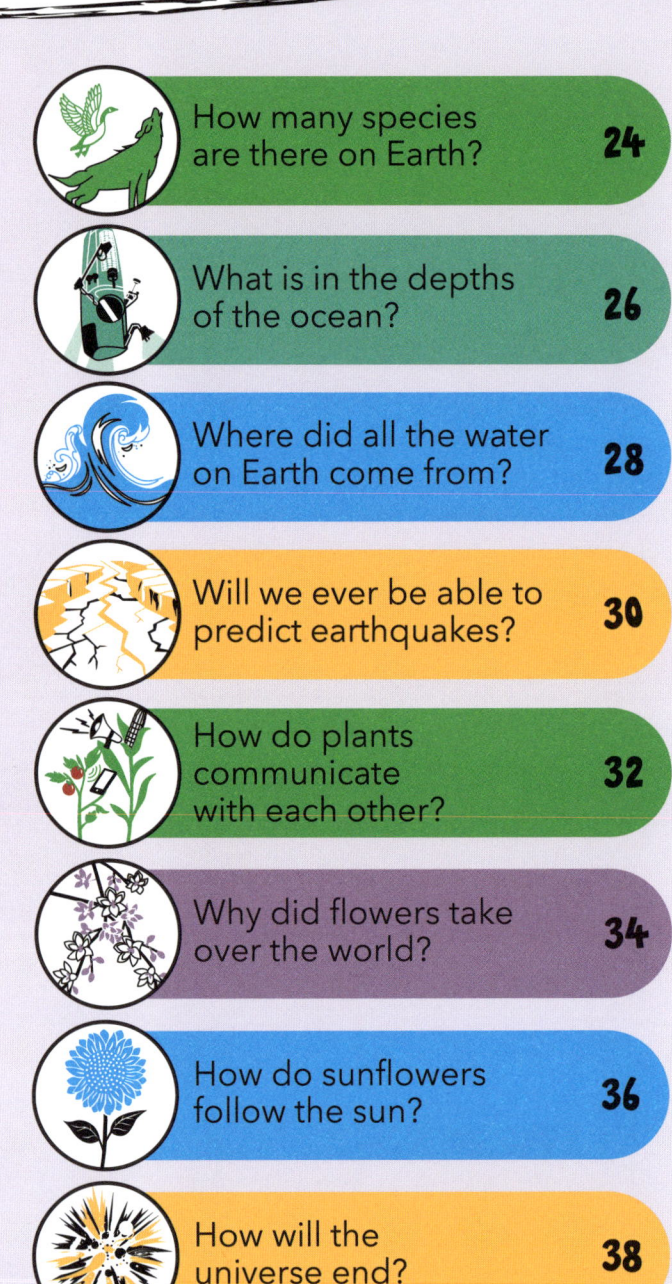

Could we ever live on another planet?	42
How fast could humans travel?	44
How big is the universe?	46
Why does gravity exist?	48
How did the moon form?	50
Why do we age?	52
Why do we laugh?	54
Why do we dream?	56
Why do we yawn?	58
Why do we get hiccups?	60
Why do we have fingerprints?	62
Why do we have an appendix?	64
How do bicycles stay upright?	66
How do airplanes stay in the air?	68
Could time travel become a reality?	70
Can we keep making faster computers?	72
Will computers become smarter than humans?	74
Glossary and Acknowledgments	76
Index	78
About the Ri and about the author	80

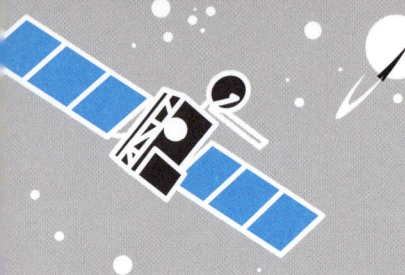

A world of SCIENTISTS

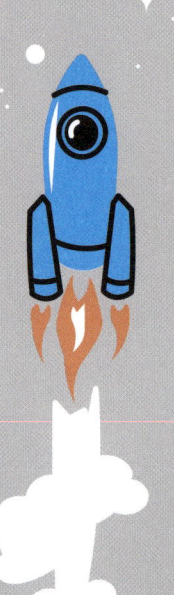

A global quest
All across the world, you will find scientists working hard to understand more about ourselves, the world around us, and the universe beyond. On every continent and in every ocean, even in the frozen darkness of Antarctica and in space, these people are trying to understand our environment and how it is changing. There are, in fact, almost 9 million scientists in the world, and this number is growing every year.

Working together
Scientists don't usually work on their own. They work with others in laboratories, or labs, and also with different teams in other labs around the world. CERN (pronounced "surn"), the research center where scientists are hunting for tiny particles, is based in Switzerland, but works with 12,000 scientists based in 70 different countries!

Standing on the shoulders of giants

Scientists also work with those who came before them. All scientists share their discoveries so that others can read and learn from their ideas. This has been happening for thousands of years, building up a giant mountain of knowledge from scientists all around the world. From the top of this mountain, we can see farther and build higher. One famous 17th-century scientist, Sir Isaac Newton, described this as "standing on the shoulders of giants".

Into the unknown

Even with this mountain of knowledge built up over thousands of years, there is still plenty we don't really understand. You may be surprised to find that many of the questions in this book explore quite simple but very important topics that you have thought about at one point or another.

Hunting for FACTS

It all starts with a question

Most scientists start off with a question. For example, what do seeds need to sprout and start growing? They then observe the world and think of possible answers. Plants grow faster in the sun or when it rains, so maybe seeds need light and water to sprout. This is called a hypothesis—not a random guess, but an idea based on a scientist's understanding of the world.

Let's experiment!

The next step is to design an experiment to test the hypothesis. We could, for example, grow seeds with and without light and water to see if they need both. We collect some dried beans, four clear water glasses or jars, and some paper towels. Set the glasses up as shown below, placing the beans at the side of the glass so we can see them. The only differences between them are the presence or absence of light and water.

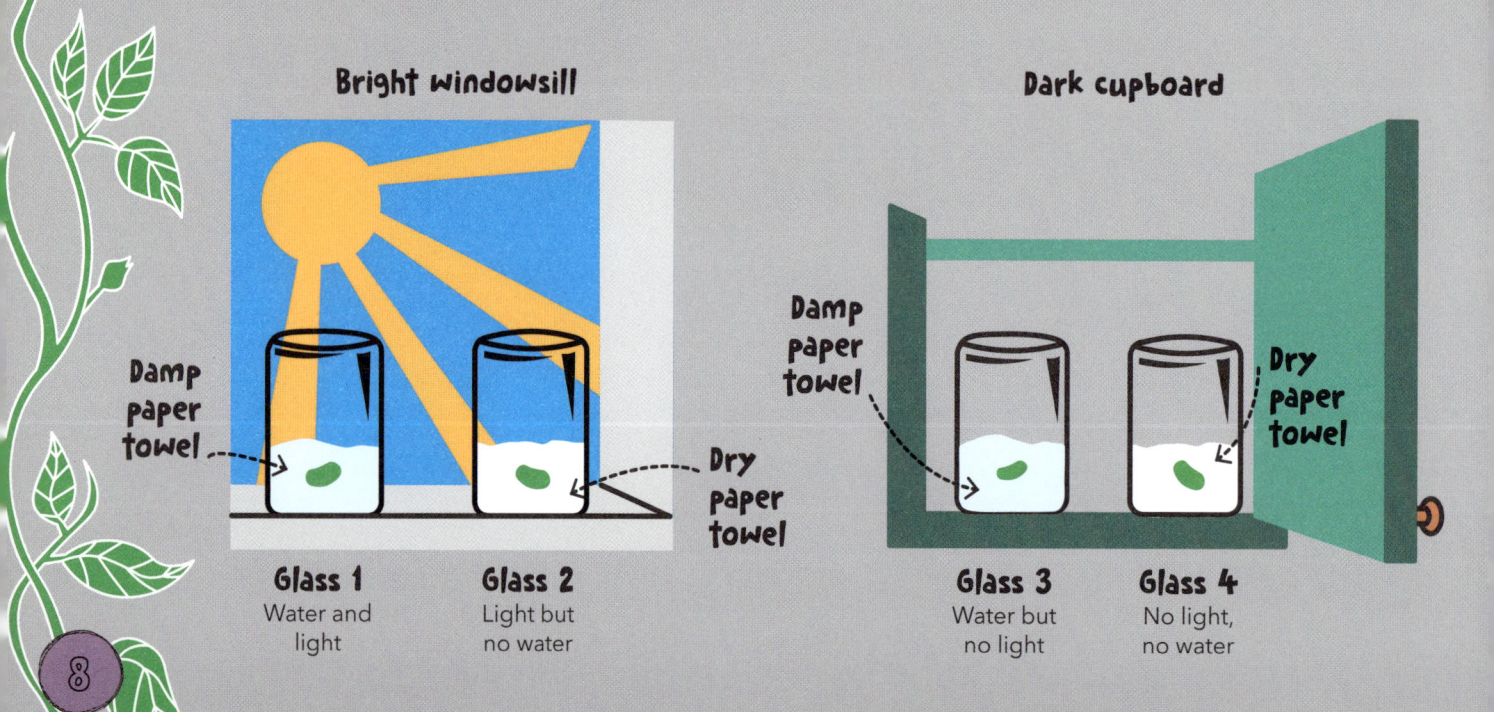

Bright windowsill

Damp paper towel

Dry paper towel

Glass 1 Water and light

Glass 2 Light but no water

Dark cupboard

Damp paper towel

Dry paper towel

Glass 3 Water but no light

Glass 4 No light, no water

Collect and analyze data

While running an experiment, scientists make careful measurements to explain what happened. For this experiment, we measure how tall the beans have grown every two days for three weeks.

Bright windowsill

Strong shoot

Glass 1
Water and light

Glass 2
Light but no water

Dark cupboard

Sprouted but sickly

Glass 3
Water but no light

Glass 4
No light, no water

Draw a conclusion

We see that the beans with water and light sprouted, but so did those with water but no light. The bean with light but no water did not sprout. Hooray—we've made a discovery! Beans need water to sprout, but not light. (They will need light to grow from now on, though.) Even if we saw no difference between some of our jars, that is still useful. We can cross one idea off, and think up another hypothesis to test.

Hunting for the truth

Many of the questions you will find in this book have more than one hypothesis to explain what is going on. Slowly, over time, scientists will find ways to test their ideas and move us slowly closer to finding out the truth. For now, read on for a journey into the unknown, and explore science at the very fringes of human knowledge and understanding!

Why are there so many BEETLES?

Goliath beetle
Males can grow up to 4.3 in (11 cm) long.

How many are there?
Scientists have counted about 1.7 million animal species so far, and **400,000 of these are beetles.** That's almost a quarter of all animals! So why are there so many?

Flower power
When the first beetles appeared around **300 million years ago,** the world was very different. Looking around the **swampy forests,** you would notice one thing missing—**flowers!** But as flowering plants evolved, they provided new **sources of food** for beetles and, in return, beetles pollinated plants. This very successful arrangement allowed them both to flourish—and expand into new **environments.**

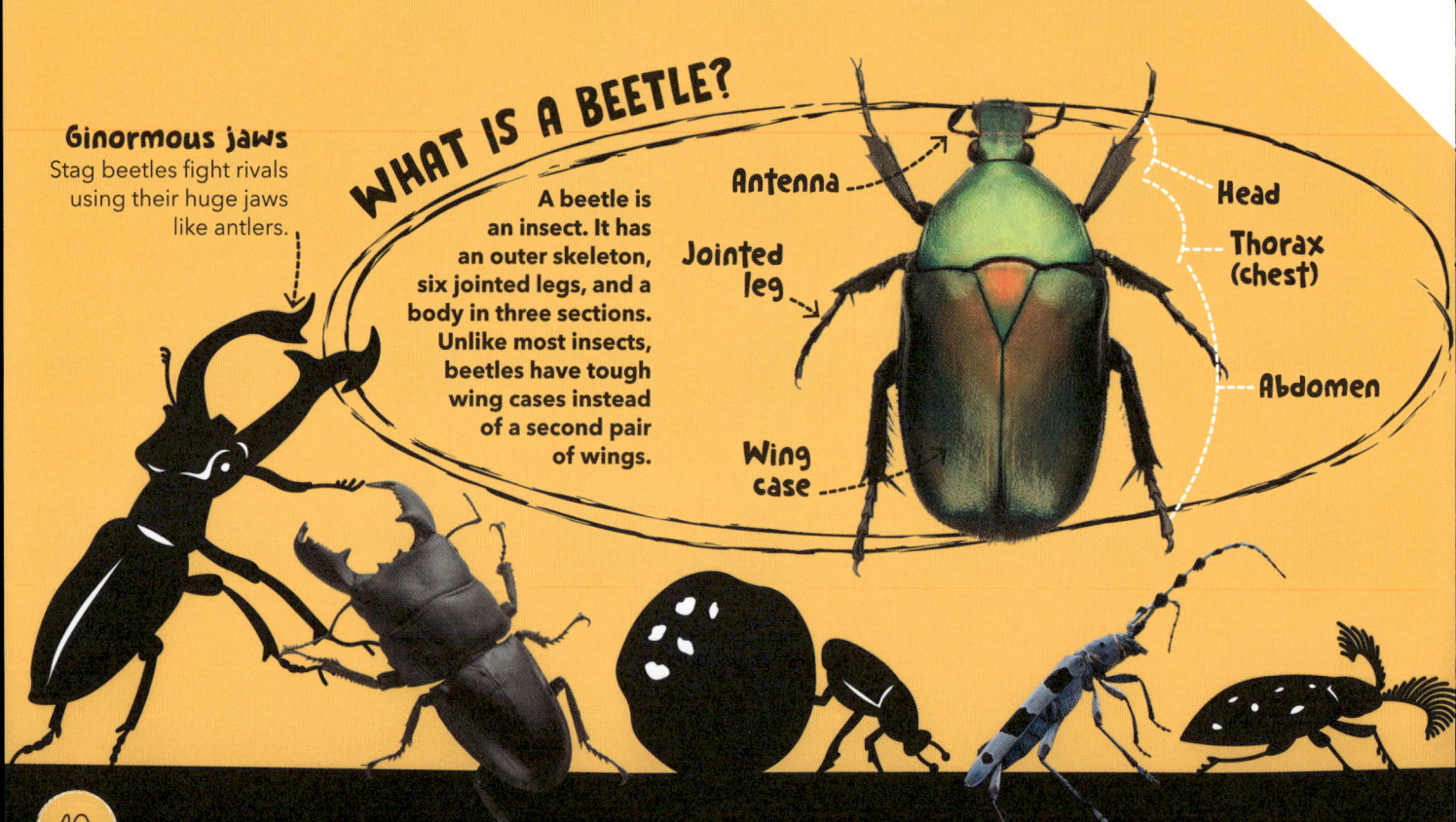

Ginormous jaws
Stag beetles fight rivals using their huge jaws like antlers.

WHAT IS A BEETLE?
A beetle is an insect. It has an outer skeleton, six jointed legs, and a body in three sections. Unlike most insects, beetles have tough wing cases instead of a second pair of wings.

- Antenna
- Jointed leg
- Wing case
- Head
- Thorax (chest)
- Abdomen

10

Want to discover a new species of animal? Look for a beetle. Scientists believe there are more than a million still to find!

Power pollinator
As beetles feed on nectar, they pick up pollen and transport it to other flowers.

Super survivors
On the other hand, perhaps beetles are just great at **not going extinct.** Did you know that 99 percent of all animal species that ever lived have gone extinct, but only **16 percent** of beetle species have died out? Since they first emerged, beetles have survived three of the five **major mass extinctions** in the history of life on Earth—including the **giant asteroid** thought to have wiped out most of the dinosaurs. But how? Is it that they are small, tough, and able to withstand extremes of hot and cold? Or is it because they are **super flexible** about the food they eat? Perhaps both? We don't know for sure.

Ladybug liftoff!
Beetles fly with their rear wings—the front pair evolved into hard protective wing cases.

Fossil clues
To find out more, scientists are studying **beetle fossils** alongside living beetles to see how, when, and why different beetles **thrived, evolved, or died** over time. Beetles play an important part in ecosystems, so this information will help us understand the **health of habitats** today.

WHY STUDY BEETLES?
Some beetles are vital pollinators, but others can be pests. Scientists work to protect food crops without killing beetles and damaging the ecosystem.

Why did the WOOLLY MAMMOTH go extinct?

The frosty giant
If you went back 20,000 years, you would find a much colder world. This was the final peak of the last ice age, and **colossal sheets of ice covered a quarter of Earth's land.** The woolly mammoth had been king of this icy world for nearly **300,000 years,** safe from the sub-zero temperatures under its thick fur. Yet within another 10,000 years, this giant was **almost extinct.** Why?

The last few mammoths survived until 4,000 years ago—after the pyramids of Egypt were built.

WHAT IS A WOOLLY MAMMOTH?
Woolly mammoths were closely related to elephants, but adapted to the cold. To reduce heat loss, they had a thick layer of fat, a double layer of fur, and small ears. They were just one of several species of mammoth at the time.

Double coat
Woolly mammoths had two layers of fur for warmth. The shaggy outer layer was up to 20 in (50 cm) long.

Multitool
Tusks were used to dig under the snow and to fight rivals.

Sole support
Large fatty pads cushioned their heels, just like in the feet of modern elephants.

The big hunt

As the last ice age ended, **humans spread** around the warming world. Our ancestors were bad news for the woolly mammoth—these skilled hunters **caught the big beasts** for food and used their tusks and fur to make tools and clothing. Maybe hungry humans **hunted them to extinction.**

Human hunters
Early humans used tools and teamwork to bring down mighty mammoths.

A changing world

At the same time, the **melting ice sheets** transformed the woolly mammoths' habitat. Dry plains gave way to rivers and wetlands, where new plants thrived and **old food sources disappeared.** They surely struggled in this rapidly changing environment—perhaps they simply **could not adapt** fast enough.

Invasive infection

As the ice melted, **species from warmer areas** moved in, bringing new germs with them. **Microbes in the ice** may also have defrosted and become active again. Scientists are searching for evidence to find out if one of these germs become **a lethal "hyperdisease"** that wiped out the mammoths.

Killer combination

It's **hard to know** if one of these factors alone proved fatal. It seems likely that a changing climate and human hunting **both cut mammoth numbers** and perhaps disease just finished them off.

WHY STUDY EXTINCT SPECIES?
Scientists hope that studying the last mammoths could help prevent elephants one day going extinct, too.

How do MONARCH BUTTERFLIES find their way?

An incredible journey

Many animals make incredible journeys each year, but one of the most impressive is **a tiny traveler**—the monarch butterfly. Every fall, as temperatures drop and the days shorten, hundreds of thousands of monarch butterflies fly **3,000 miles (4,800 km) south** from the US and Canada to warmer Mexico. None of them has ever made this journey before, yet somehow **they know where to go.**

When they need to cross the ocean, monarch butterflies wait for a strong wind to help them fly safely across.

Follow the sun

Monarchs only fly during the day, so it could be that they **use the sun to navigate.** By looking at the sun's position during the day, it's possible to figure out roughly **which direction is south.** But what about cloudy days?

Magnetic skills

The Earth's core is essentially a giant magnet. Around this is **an invisible magnetic field, which birds can detect** and use to figure out where north and south are. Recent research suggests that **monarchs may have the same ability,** using the magnetic field as well as the sun to guide their path.

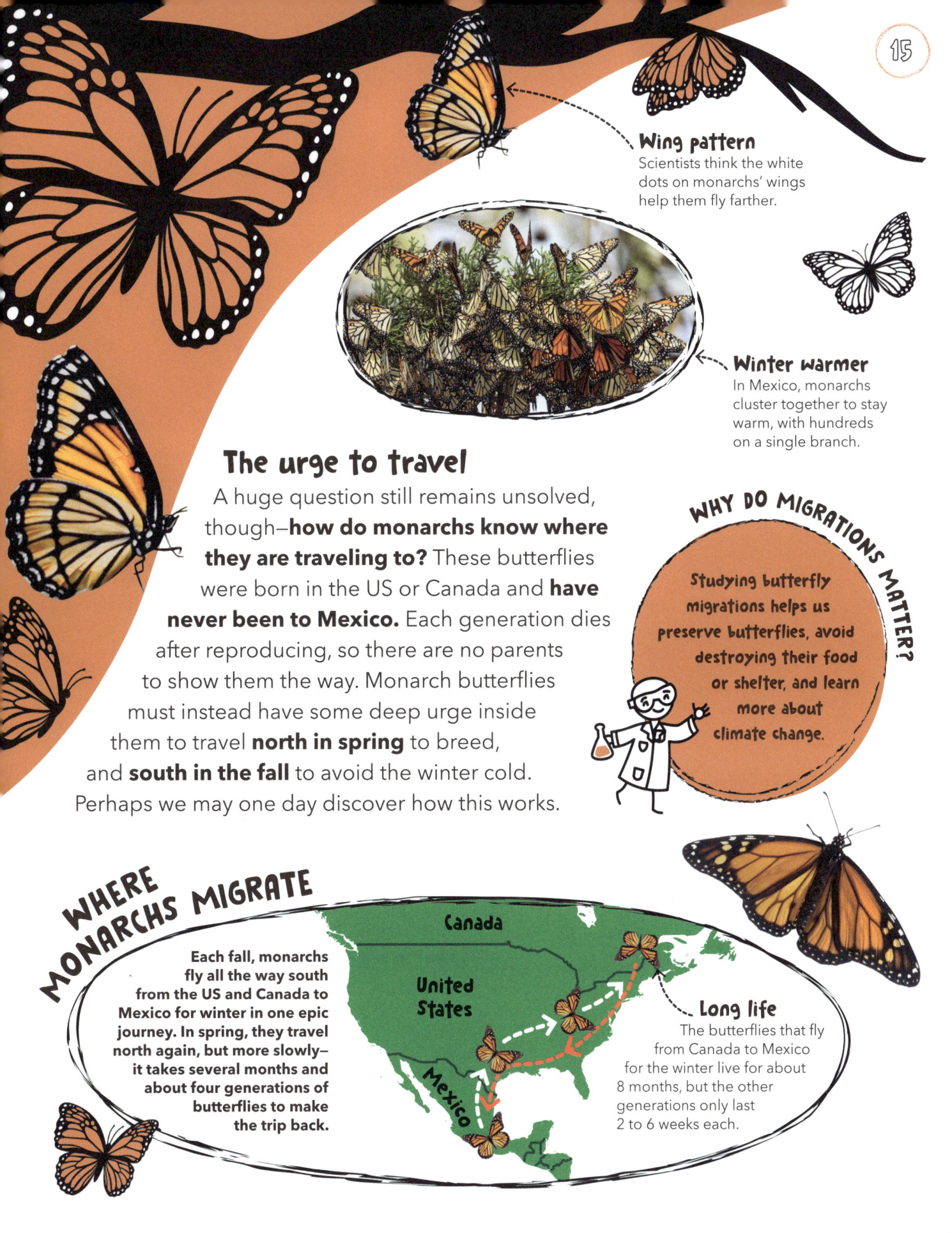

Wing pattern
Scientists think the white dots on monarchs' wings help them fly farther.

Winter warmer
In Mexico, monarchs cluster together to stay warm, with hundreds on a single branch.

The urge to travel
A huge question still remains unsolved, though—**how do monarchs know where they are traveling to?** These butterflies were born in the US or Canada and **have never been to Mexico.** Each generation dies after reproducing, so there are no parents to show them the way. Monarch butterflies must instead have some deep urge inside them to travel **north in spring** to breed, and **south in the fall** to avoid the winter cold. Perhaps we may one day discover how this works.

WHY DO MIGRATIONS MATTER?
Studying butterfly migrations helps us preserve butterflies, avoid destroying their food or shelter, and learn more about climate change.

WHERE MONARCHS MIGRATE
Each fall, monarchs fly all the way south from the US and Canada to Mexico for winter in one epic journey. In spring, they travel north again, but more slowly—it takes several months and about four generations of butterflies to make the trip back.

Long life
The butterflies that fly from Canada to Mexico for the winter live for about 8 months, but the other generations only last 2 to 6 weeks each.

Why did the STEGOSAURUS have plates?

Spiky tail
The four spikes near the end of its tail are called a "thagomizer".

Mighty Stegosaurus

The Stegosaurus is one of the most well-known dinosaurs, and **for good reason!** It towered over most land animals alive today, while the **rows of giant plates** running down its back and the spikes at the end of its long tail make it **instantly recognizable.** But why did it wear these **bony backplates**—for protection, to show off, or to shed heat?

Armor plated

As a plant-eater, the Stegosaurus would have spent much of the day feeding, and its plates could have helped it **stay safe from attack.** For a start, they made the Stegosaurus appear much larger than it was, **scaring off attackers.** And even if a predator did try to strike, the **sharp-edged plates** and spiky tail club would help **mount a fierce defense.**

Big beast
The Stegosaurus was as tall as an elephant and almost as long as a London bus.

For a big dinosaur, the Stegosaurus had a small brain—it was about the size of a lemon!

Social dinosaurs

Defense makes sense, but that theory ignores the **complex social life** Stegosauruses likely had. It's possible these plates were **covered in brightly colored skin** that could change color. If so, the plates might have helped individuals recognize their friends, send signals to each other, or even put on **a showy display** like a peacock fanning its tail.

Rush of blood
Stegosaurus plates may have turned red when excited and helped to attract a mate.

PUTTING FLESH ON THE BONES

Most dinosaur remains are fossilized bones. To figure out what muscles they had and how they moved, scientists look at the size of the bones and at scars where muscles attached. They also compare these with living reptiles and birds.

Stegosaurus fossil

Keeping cool

Some well-preserved fossils show that Stegosaurus plates had a **complex network of blood vessels** on their surface. This has led some scientists to suggest these plates also helped these dinosaurs **keep cool by radiating heat—** just as an African elephant does with its big ears!

WHY STUDY DINOSAURS?

Dinosaurs were alive for 165 million years—their remains help us piece together information about evolution and the Earth over a vast period of time.

An unsolvable mystery

Without seeing a **living Stegosaurus,** we can never know the true purpose of the plates. As they went extinct **more than 100 million years ago,** that won't be possible—unless someone invents a time machine!

Why do things keep EVOLVING INTO CRABS?

A marine mystery

Crabs are part of a group called **crustaceans,** together with shrimp and lobsters, but they have a **very different body shape** from these cousins. The long abdomen you see in shrimp and lobsters is tucked under the belly in crabs, whose whole body is **flat and round.** True crabs evolved this form about 300 million years ago, but since then **five other groups** of crustaceans have developed similar crab-shaped bodies – these groups are known as false crabs. Why do **so many paths** lead to crabs?

The Japanese Spider Crab is the largest in the world, with a legspan of up to 13 ft (4 m)!

Crabby long-legs
Spider crabs' long legs help these hunters climb around rocky islands and seafloors.

TRUE AND FALSE CRABS

Blue crab

True crab
True crabs have four pairs of walking legs plus one pair of claws. Their body is flat, wide, and in one piece.

False crab
These crustaceans are called crabs and look like crabs, but they are imposters! They have a rounder body and only three pairs of walking legs.

Porcelain crab

The benefits of being a crab

The **process of evolution** makes animals **better suited** to their environments. So if the crab-shape has evolved so many times there must be something **really good** about it. Some scientists suggest that this shape makes animals **better at hiding** from predators—the flat shell helps them tuck under rocks, and the sideways scuttle is a **quick way to escape.** Their abdomen is also safely tucked away and **protected from any predator.**

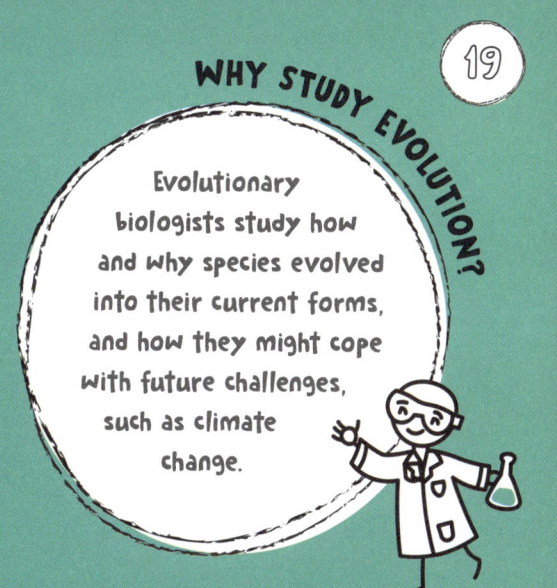

WHY STUDY EVOLUTION?

Evolutionary biologists study how and why species evolved into their current forms, and how they might cope with future challenges, such as climate change.

Crab-daptable

There are more than **7,000 species** of crab, with a range of **specialities:** some can dig with their back legs, others have flat paddlelike legs for swimming (see the blue crab opposite) and many have **huge claws for fighting!** Maybe the crab's compact shape is simply a body plan that makes **a great base for adapting** to different environments.

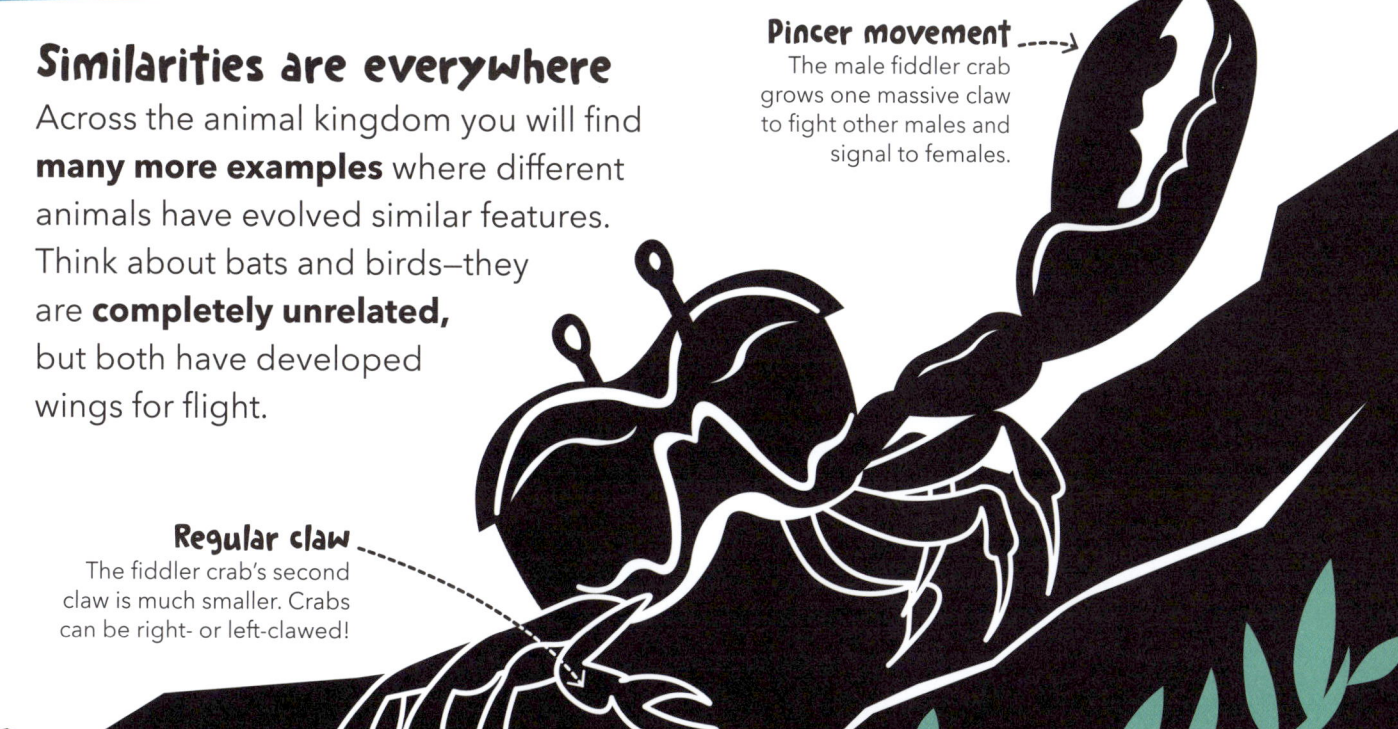

Similarities are everywhere

Across the animal kingdom you will find **many more examples** where different animals have evolved similar features. Think about bats and birds—they are **completely unrelated,** but both have developed wings for flight.

Pincer movement
The male fiddler crab grows one massive claw to fight other males and signal to females.

Regular claw
The fiddler crab's second claw is much smaller. Crabs can be right- or left-clawed!

Why do ANIMALS NEED SLEEP?

Kingdom of snooze

From whales to weevils, **almost every animal sleeps.** Most humans sleep safely in houses that protect us, but out in the wild, **sleeping animals are very vulnerable** to being eaten. Sleep also takes up time that could be spent feeding, mating, or socializing. This means that **sleep must be very important**—otherwise animals would never have evolved this **risky behavior.**

Personal pillow
Giraffes can nap while standing, but lie down with their head on their body for a real snooze.

Time to sleep

To a scientist, sleep means **being still in one position** and not responding to external disturbances, but still being able to wake up quickly if needed. Among mammals, **larger animals tend to sleep less.** Scientists think this is because they have to spend so much time **eating food** to fuel their **giant bodies.** An elephant, for example, only sleeps about two hours a day!

WHAT HAPPENS WHEN WE SLEEP

There is a lot going on inside your body while you sleep. As well as resting, it is cleaning and repairing itself, to be ready for the next day.

Brain
Cells store memories and clean up harmful chemicals.

Lungs
Your breathing becomes slower and shallower.

Muscles
Your muscles relax and you move far less.

Digestive system
Special bacteria become active and clean the gut while you sleep.

Benefitting the brain

Sleep is very important for the brain. When we sleep, it can focus on **storing memories** from the day without distraction. Our bodies can also get rid of **waste chemicals** and restore the brain's **energy supplies**—crucial for humans since our brains use about 20 percent of our energy. But there is **one key problem** with this theory—not all animals have brains!

> Dolphins and whales only sleep with one side of their brain at a time, allowing them to come up to the surface to breathe while asleep.

Whole body sleep

Jellyfish don't have a brain, but have been **observed sleeping.** Scientists therefore suggest that sleep might allow energy to be used for other jobs around the body, such as **growth, repairing damage, and digesting food.** This is the case in humans, since sleeping **reduces the energy** our bodies are using.

Hang time
Bats sleep upside-down to save energy. When they relax their legs, their claws lock onto the tree without using any muscles.

Simple slumber
Jellyfish don't have a brain—just a simple ring of nerves. And yet they too enter an inactive state resembling sleep.

Essential evolution

Whatever its primary purpose, sleep likely evolved more than **500 million years ago,** in the first simple animals, and so it must be **one of the most vital parts of animal life.** This is worth remembering if you need to convince anyone to let you sleep in a little longer!

WHY STUDY SLEEP?
Studying sleep across all species helps scientists protect animals from human light and noise pollution. It can also shed light on human sleep disorders.

How did LIFE BEGIN?

The birth of Earth
When planet Earth formed about 4.5 billion years ago, it was a **hot and violent world.** Active volcanoes covered its surface, and a nonstop barrage of meteors **crashed down from space.** Yet less than a billion years later, the earliest forms of life emerged in this chaotic landscape. **Everything alive today,** from a potato to a penguin, traces back to this amazing era.

Finding the recipe
How can we figure out how life began? Some scientists think the key is to understand the environment back then. **Life definitely evolved in water,** and by testing fossilized rocks from this period, we can see what **chemical substances** were around. Scientists are combining these in the laboratory and **trying to make life.** They have not yet succeeded, but have produced some **small molecules** that are found inside living cells today.

Some scientists think the molecules needed to form life came from the thousands of meteorites bombarding the young planet Earth.

The spark of life
To create life takes more than just the **right chemical substances**—you also need energy! Scientists think this energy could have come from **lightning strikes.** Or perhaps the heat of Earth's core helped life evolve near **superhot jets of water** erupting from the seafloor.

Volcanic vents
Water heated deep in the ground emerges through breaks in the seabed called fissures or vents. Today they teem with life.

22

Living soup

The best idea we have so far is that around **3.6 billion years ago,** Earth was covered in a hot "soup" of water, filled with a complex mix of chemical substances. Maybe powered by heat from Earth's volcanoes, **these molecules started to produce copies of each other.** In time, they clumped together into blobs, making the first cells. This process either took hundreds of millions of years, or just a few, depending on who you ask! All we know for sure is that **an early organism** with multiple cells was living on Earth by **1.6 billion years ago.**

Stromatolites
Tiny early organisms grew together in sticky mats that trapped minerals from the water to form rocks called stromatolites.

WHAT IS LIFE?

The most basic lifeforms are single-celled organisms—each a tiny bag of liquid holding the materials to feed, grow, and reproduce. Many of these are bacteria, which make up three-quarters of all living species today. What came before these remains a mystery.

Volcanoes
Hot lava and gases from inside Earth may have supplied minerals and energy for early life.

Bacterium
Bacteria are living organisms made up of just one cell.

WHY STUDY THE ORIGINS OF LIFE?

Learning more about how life began helps scientists predict whether life might exist on other planets, and how to find it.

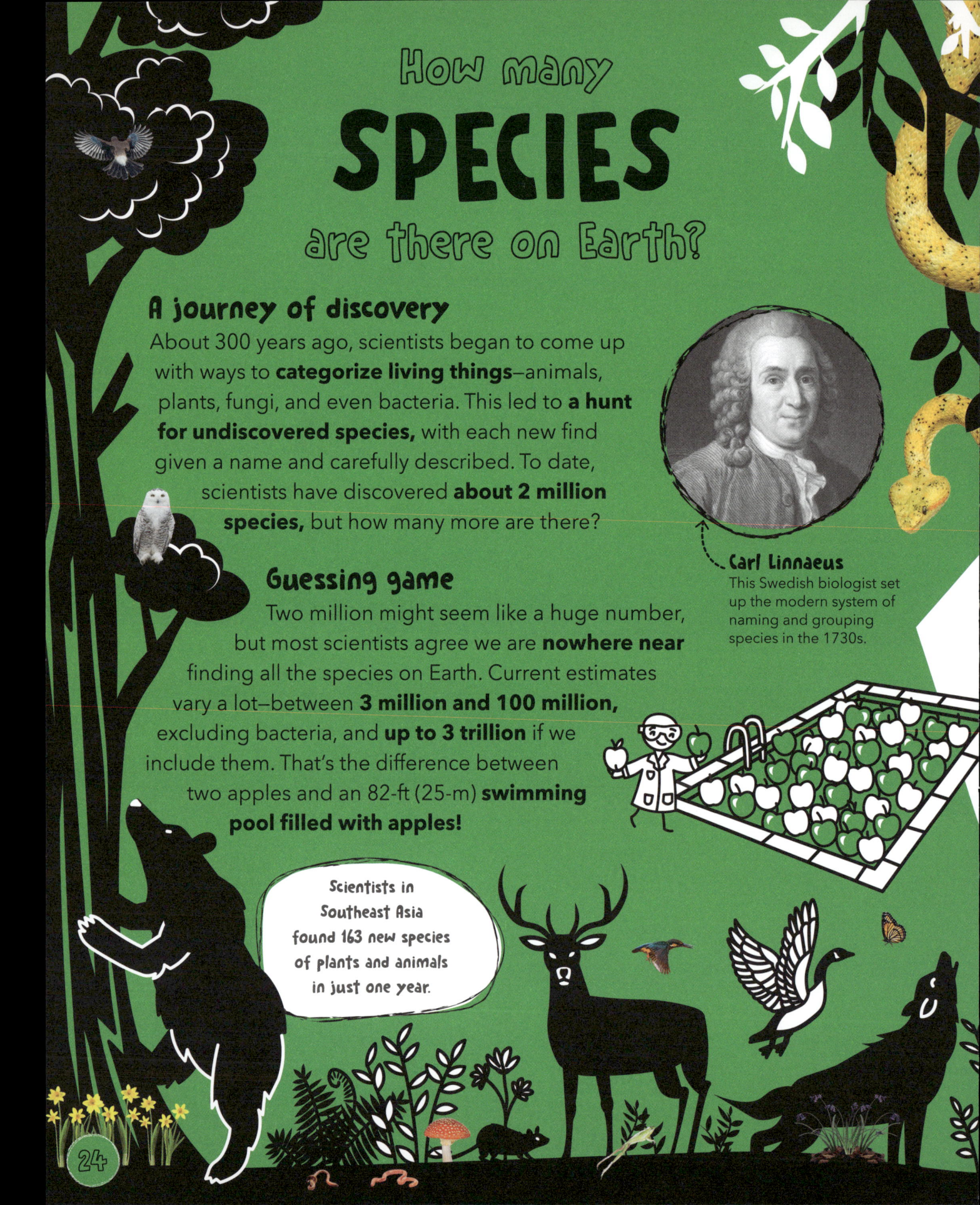

How many SPECIES are there on Earth?

A journey of discovery
About 300 years ago, scientists began to come up with ways to **categorize living things**—animals, plants, fungi, and even bacteria. This led to **a hunt for undiscovered species,** with each new find given a name and carefully described. To date, scientists have discovered **about 2 million species,** but how many more are there?

Carl Linnaeus
This Swedish biologist set up the modern system of naming and grouping species in the 1730s.

Guessing game
Two million might seem like a huge number, but most scientists agree we are **nowhere near** finding all the species on Earth. Current estimates vary a lot—between **3 million and 100 million,** excluding bacteria, and **up to 3 trillion** if we include them. That's the difference between two apples and an 82-ft (25-m) **swimming pool filled with apples!**

> Scientists in Southeast Asia found 163 new species of plants and animals in just one year.

Family paw-trait
There are 359 different dog breeds, but they are all one species.

What is a species?

An even bigger problem is **defining what a species is.** It's not just a group of organisms that look the same—dogs can look very different, yet are **all the same species!** Most scientists would say that organisms that can **breed together and make babies** are the same species. But some animals, including the whiptail lizard, can make babies on their own, without needing a mate.

COUNTING SPECIES IN AN AREA

To estimate the number of species in a large area, choose a few smaller sample areas and count the species in those. When new searches stop finding new species, we have probably found most of them!

Setting up
Each search area is marked out with string, or using a square frame called a quadrat.

Sample area

Count them before they're gone

We will never know exactly how many species there are, but **we can certainly improve our estimate.** Humans have spread across the world, but there are many mountains, jungles, caves, and oceans still unexplored. **More and more species go extinct each year,** so many have likely disappeared without ever being discovered. We should try to **find and preserve** as many as we can before they are gone.

WHY COUNT SPECIES?

Counting species regularly helps us spot when the environment is in trouble—losing just a few species can collapse an entire food chain.

Dodo
The last of these large, flightless birds was seen alive in 1662.

What is in the depths of the OCEAN?

Snailfish
Some species of snailfish live as deep as 26,250 ft (8,000 m) below sea level.

The great unknown
The lowest point of the ocean is the Challenger Deep, a staggering **36,037 ft (10,984 m) below sea level**—that's far deeper than Mount Everest is tall! Even at a tenth of that depth, the crushing pressure, **near-freezing cold,** and total darkness of the deep ocean make venturing there **more dangerous than space travel.**

Life in the deep
Scientists once thought that little could survive in the deep ocean—there is **no light** for plants to make food, and **the pressure** would **crush most creatures.** Yet, after exploring only 5 percent of these depths, scientists have found a **surprising number of living things,** many of them very weird indeed.

Super sub
Submersibles are designed to resist the huge pressures of the deep ocean.

Searchlight
Bright lights attract curious creatures and reveal the deep sea's surprising secrets.

THE BOTTOM OF THE OCEAN
The seafloor is shallow near the coast, and then drops down to ocean basins far from land. These basins are about 12,000 ft (3,700 m) deep on average, but contain long, narrow trenches that are much deeper.

- Shallow coast
- Ocean basin
- Trench

Weird wonders

The **sea pig** is a typical deep-sea animal, spending its time slowly browsing the sea floor for **scraps of food** that have fallen from above. Like many deep dwellers, it has **a transparent body to avoid being eaten.** The anglerfish, in contrast, wants to be seen—it attracts prey with a **brightly glowing blob** over its mouth!

Secretive squids

Perhaps the most infamous creatures of the deep are **the elusive giant squid** and its even rarer cousin, the **colossal squid.** For years the only traces of them were **strange scars on whales,** and later a few dead squid. Adult colossal squid have **never been seen** in their natural habitat, and scientists are still not sure quite how big they can grow—one bus length or two?

Alien landscapes

Some of the strangest finds so far on the ocean floor are **giant natural chimneys** that belch out superhot mineral-rich water. These support **an entire network of life** without energy from the sun. Bacteria digest minerals in the water, providing food for 10-ft (3-m) long worms, **blind crabs,** and more. All these amazing discoveries have been made in **just a fraction of the deep ocean—** imagine what else is out there!

The pressure at the deepest point of the ocean would feel like having 100 elephants standing on your head!

Luminous lure
A female anglerfish attracts prey with a light, then swallows it whole.

Giant tube worms
Bacteria inside the worms turn sulfur in the water into energy.

Finger food
Yeti crabs grow edible bacteria on their claws.

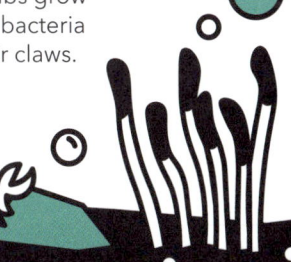

WHY EXPLORE OCEAN DEPTHS?
Scientists think that exploring the deep ocean may help us learn about earthquakes, how life survives extreme conditions, and perhaps even the origins of life.

Where did all the WATER ON EARTH come from?

A dry start

Our solar system formed from a cloud of dust and gas, which **clumped together** to form the planets we know today. On the distant edges of the solar system, **crystals of frozen water** were probably abundant, but closer to the sun where Earth formed, any water **quickly evaporated.** Our planet therefore started life dry and hot. So where did our water come from?

Scientists think there could be at least as much water locked inside Earth's rocks as there is in the oceans.

Scorched Earth
Early Earth was far too hot for surface water to form.

Volcanic origins

Some scientists suggest that the water on Earth was made here. Early Earth was **covered in volcanoes** and vast **oceans of molten rock.** These would have been hot enough for oxygen in these rocks to react with hydrogen in the atmosphere to form water. **More water** could have formed as rocks melted deep in the Earth, allowing **hydrogen and oxygen** in different rocks to combine.

Fire and water
Surprisingly, one of the most common volcanic gases is water vapor.

A gift from outer space

Beyond Jupiter, you can find many **space rocks packed full of frozen water.** Early in its existence, Earth was constantly bombarded with these rocks—you can see evidence of this in the moon's crater-filled surface. It could be that these **icy bodies** delivered a plentiful supply of water to turn our planet into the **water-world** it is today.

Rocky rain
Today most rocks burn up in Earth's atmosphere.

WHAT IS WATER?

Hydrogen
Pure hydrogen is rare on Earth.

Oxygen
Oxygen makes up 21 percent of the air we breathe.

The chemical symbol for water is H_2O—two hydrogen atoms bonded to one oxygen. It forms when these two elements combine in a chemical reaction, releasing energy.

Water-world
Seen from space, Earth looks like a blue marble.

WHY STUDY THE ORIGINS OF WATER?

Water is vital to life on Earth, and perhaps on other planets too. Wherever liquid water exists, there may also be life.

The answer is out there

Using increasingly powerful telescopes, we have started to find **signs of water** on planets in **distant galaxies.** Observing their oceans, each at a different stage of development, could help us understand where ours came from. All life on Earth relies on water to survive so, however it got here, we should be **thankful** for our **watery home.**

Will we ever be able to PREDICT EARTHQUAKES?

Earth-shaking issues

Earthquakes are deadly natural disasters, affecting millions of people across the planet. When **the ground buckles and shakes,** it can break gas pipes causing fires, destroy whole buildings, and even trigger **giant, destructive ocean waves.** Scientists understand clearly what causes earthquakes, but figuring out **exactly when** they're going to happen is currently impossible.

In countries such as Japan where earthquakes are common, skyscrapers are built on rubber bases to absorb some of the wobbles.

What causes earthquakes?

Earth's surface is a jigsaw of thin plates floating on a layer of slow-moving, superhot rock. The borders between plates are called fault lines. When these plates bump and slide against each other, they release huge bursts of energy that make the ground shake.

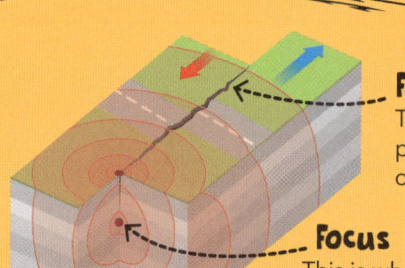

Fault line
Two plates slide past each other in opposite directions.

Focus
This is where tension gives way below ground, causing violent vibrations.

Bad vibrations
Taller buildings are more vulnerable to violent shaking.

Shock absorber
The Transamerica Pyramid in San Francisco is designed to survive earthquakes.

Finding patterns

Since the 1900s, scientists across the world have recorded the **time and location** of earthquakes. This data might show that a strong earthquake happens in the same city roughly every 100 years, but it **can't predict** the **specific year** when one will happen. But noticing patterns is still useful to identify areas where earthquakes happen a lot, so engineers can design buildings to **withstand the shaking.**

30

Looking for clues

To help make predictions, scientists are looking for things that happen **just before an earthquake** occurs. For example, does part of the Earth bulge outward, or does its **magnetic field** change? Do **gases leak** out of cracks as an earthquake is building up, and **can animals sense** the coming disaster? The evidence is still unclear.

Toad away!
In Italy, toads left an area shortly before an earthquake hit—did they know?

Earthquake drill
In areas with regular earthquakes, people practice how to stay safe when the ground starts shaking.

Computers to the rescue

Today, there are millions of sensors placed across the world detecting earthquakes. Computers are searching through this **mountain of data,** trying to find ways to predict exactly when an earthquake might be coming. At present, **monitoring stations** in Japan can detect the first ripples of an earthquake and give **a few minutes' notice** of the likely location and intensity. Perhaps scientists will one day be able to **extend that warning** to hours or even days ahead, as they can for some volcanic eruptions.

Earth-shattering
During an earthquake, pulses of energy travel through the earth like waves at sea, making it bend or crack.

WHY STUDY EARTHQUAKES?

Just a few hours' warning before big earthquakes could give people time to take shelter, helping to save thousands of lives a year.

How do plants COMMUNICATE with each other?

Communicating to survive

Plants can't move like animals do, yet have many survival tactics. They grow toward sunlight and nutrients, and **release chemicals** to fight off pests. But these measures take time, so **advance warning** from nearby plants is a big advantage. How do they share this important information?

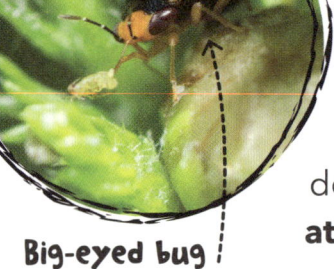

Smelly messages

If you have ever smelled **freshly cut grass,** then you've experienced a plant communicating. This special smell signals that the grass is being eaten or damaged, so nearby plants produce **toxic or foul-tasting chemicals** to deter hungry animals. Some plants' smells even **attract predators** such as wasps or bugs, which eat the insects nibbling on the leaves!

Big-eyed bug
This bug can smell when its prey is feeding nearby.

Water warning
Dry tomato plants make high-pitched popping noises.

Plant chat

Some scientists think that plants might also talk using sounds! They discovered that tomato plants produce **clicking noises,** far too high-pitched for human ears to detect. The plants made these sounds more often when they **needed water** or were **damaged,** which might act as a warning for other plants—but we don't know for sure.

32

Underground network

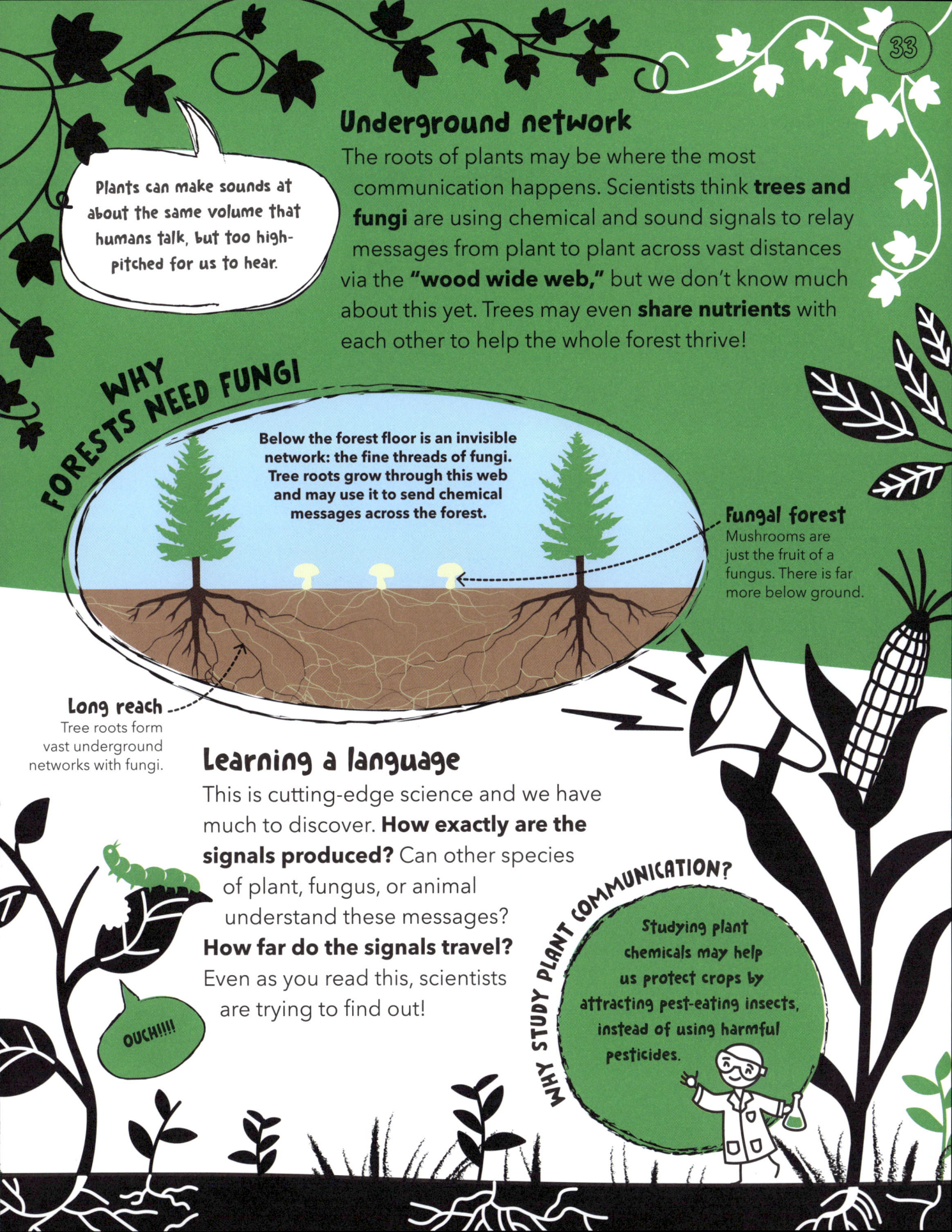

The roots of plants may be where the most communication happens. Scientists think **trees and fungi** are using chemical and sound signals to relay messages from plant to plant across vast distances via the **"wood wide web,"** but we don't know much about this yet. Trees may even **share nutrients** with each other to help the whole forest thrive!

> Plants can make sounds at about the same volume that humans talk, but too high-pitched for us to hear.

WHY FORESTS NEED FUNGI

Below the forest floor is an invisible network: the fine threads of fungi. Tree roots grow through this web and may use it to send chemical messages across the forest.

Fungal forest
Mushrooms are just the fruit of a fungus. There is far more below ground.

Long reach
Tree roots form vast underground networks with fungi.

Learning a language

This is cutting-edge science and we have much to discover. **How exactly are the signals produced?** Can other species of plant, fungus, or animal understand these messages? **How far do the signals travel?** Even as you read this, scientists are trying to find out!

OUCH!!!!

WHY STUDY PLANT COMMUNICATION?

Studying plant chemicals may help us protect crops by attracting pest-eating insects, instead of using harmful pesticides.

Why did FLOWERS take over the world?

Late bloomers

Plants began to grow on land 500 million years ago. By the time dinosaurs dominated the world, 245 million years ago, **huge forests of conifers and tree ferns** towered over all but the tallest titanosaurs. The first flowers, however, evolved **far later,** a mere 150 million years ago—yet today they make up **80 percent of all living plants.** Flowers are clearly useful to plants today, but which feature was most important in their early success?

Cycad
These ancient plants evolved long before flowers. They release pollen from their central cone.

A better way to reproduce

Instead of releasing pollen in the wind, as pine trees do, the first flowers made **nectar** that attracted insects. When these entered a flower to drink, they got covered in **sticky pollen.** They then transferred it to other flowers as they fed. This was more effective than **scattering pollen** to the wind in the hope some would land on another plant.

Deliver-bee
Bees transfer pollen between flowers as they collect nectar.

There are 235,000 known species of flowering plant in the world—that's 95 percent of all plant species!

HOW FLOWERS WORK

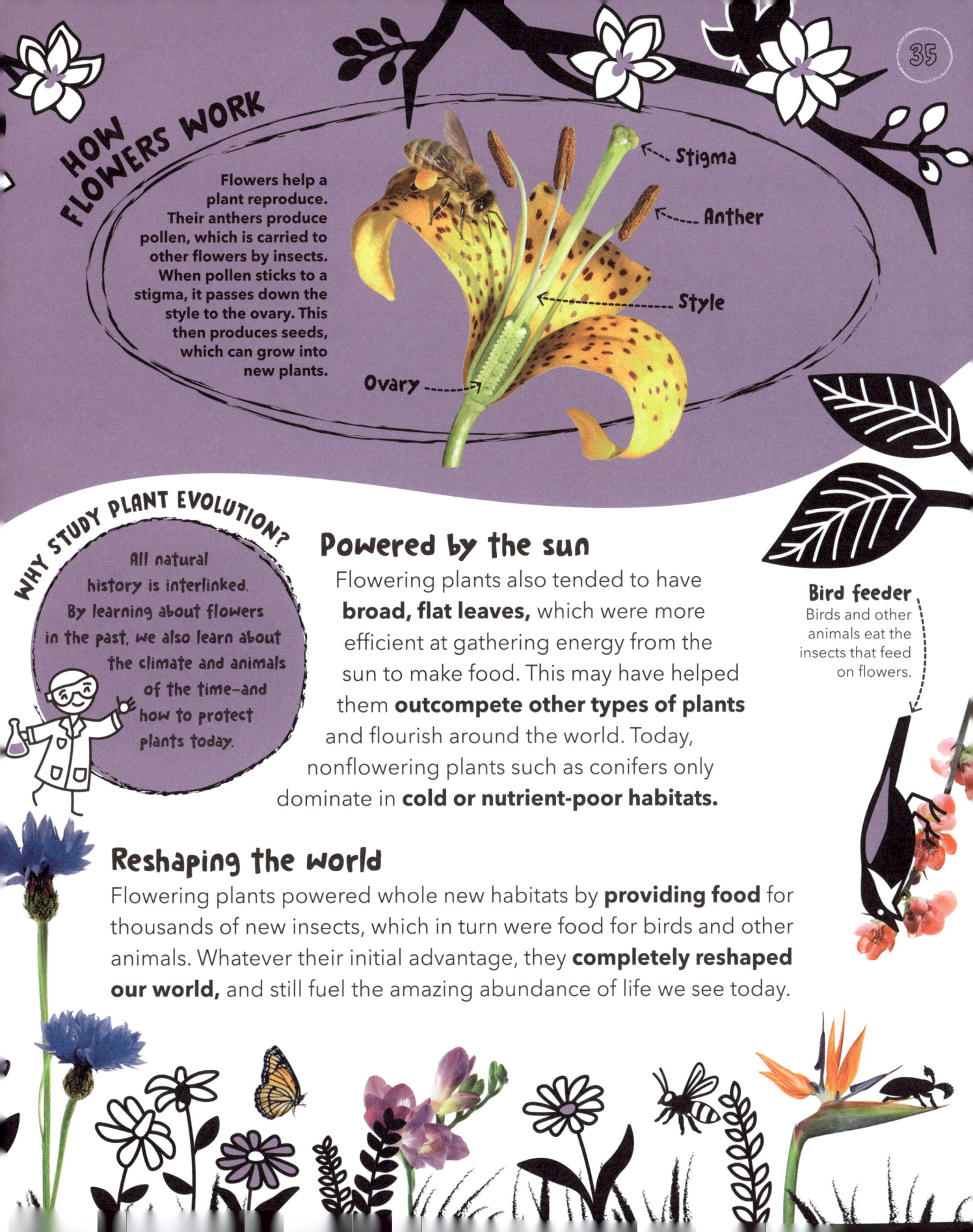

Flowers help a plant reproduce. Their anthers produce pollen, which is carried to other flowers by insects. When pollen sticks to a stigma, it passes down the style to the ovary. This then produces seeds, which can grow into new plants.

← Stigma
← Anther
← Style
Ovary

WHY STUDY PLANT EVOLUTION?
All natural history is interlinked. By learning about flowers in the past, we also learn about the climate and animals of the time—and how to protect plants today.

Powered by the sun
Flowering plants also tended to have **broad, flat leaves,** which were more efficient at gathering energy from the sun to make food. This may have helped them **outcompete other types of plants** and flourish around the world. Today, nonflowering plants such as conifers only dominate in **cold or nutrient-poor habitats.**

Bird feeder
Birds and other animals eat the insects that feed on flowers.

Reshaping the world
Flowering plants powered whole new habitats by **providing food** for thousands of new insects, which in turn were food for birds and other animals. Whatever their initial advantage, they **completely reshaped our world,** and still fuel the amazing abundance of life we see today.

How do SUNFLOWERS follow the sun?

Warm dawn
Full-grown sunflowers face east all day—only the young ones turn.

Turning heads

If you have ever seen a **field full of sunflowers,** you might have noticed they look **a little more organized** than other plants. All the heads face in one direction. If the sunflowers are still growing and you **stayed for the whole day,** you would be more surprised, observing the sunflowers **gradually tilt to stay facing the sun** as it moves across the sky.

Following the sun

Rising sun

Morning
The west side of the stem is slightly longer, which causes the young flower to lean east, toward the rising sun.

Midday
During the day, the east side of the stem grows faster. By noon, the two sides are equal, so the stem is straight and the flower faces up at the midday sun overhead.

Setting sun

Evening
The east side of the stem continues to grow until dusk. At night, the west side grows faster to tilt the bud east, ready for morning.

Push and pull
Recent experiments have **unlocked how this happens.** Scientists drew equally spaced dots on the east and west sides of the plant stem, then monitored how the gaps between the dots **changed over time.** This showed that in daylight the east side of the plant grows faster, **tilting the flower head from east to west** to track the sun. At night, the west side takes over, turning the flower east.

Like clockwork
Amazingly, scientists think sunflowers can **control their growth** using both an internal "clock" and an ability to detect the **amount of sunlight** and the **temperature,** using these to work out what time of day it is.

Controlling growth
Exactly how sunflowers grow faster on one side is the final piece of the puzzle. Plants produce special **chemicals to encourage growth** in certain parts of their bodies. These can respond to light and even gravity—a plant's first shoots **grow up toward the sun,** while its roots sink down into the soil. Scientists are trying to figure out which chemicals give the sunflower its **sun-tracking superpower.**

WHY STUDY SUNFLOWERS?
Scientists have grown sunflowers in space! Testing plants in extreme conditions helps us to keep them healthy on Earth.

Keeping time
Sunflowers know when and where the morning sun will appear.

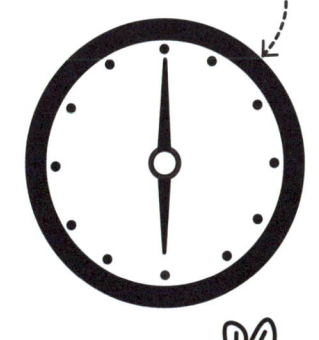

Bees visit the warmest flowers, so scientists think sunflowers may face the morning sun to heat up and attract more pollinators.

How will the UNIVERSE END?

Small beginnings

We're pretty sure that the universe started with the **Big Bang.** At that moment 13.8 billion years ago, everything that makes up our universe is thought to have **exploded into existence** from a tiny point in space—and today it is still expanding. How the universe will end, though, is much less certain.

Big Crunch
One day, gravity may pull everything back together again.

Big Bang
The name Big Bang began as a joke, but then it stuck!

EXPANDING SPACE

Most galaxies are moving away from each other. This is because space itself is expanding, which means that distant objects are getting farther away from us all the time.

Present day
The space between the galaxies has increased.

Early universe
Galaxies were once close together.

Tearaway galaxy
This galaxy is being torn apart by the gravity of a massive nearby object.

The Big Rip

The expansion of the universe is getting **faster and faster,** driven by a mysterious force called **"dark energy".** Some scientists think this could eventually **tear the universe to pieces.** First, it would pull large galaxies apart, then stars, planets, and even the very atoms that make up everything. Scientists don't know exactly **what dark energy is,** or **how it works,** so we have no idea how likely the Big Rip is!

The Big Freeze

Another option is that, as the universe continues to expand, material gradually becomes so **thinly spread** over such vast areas that the temperature drops to just above **absolute zero** (-460°F or -273°C). This is the lowest possible temperature, because at this point **all matter stops moving.** With no motion or activity, the universe is essentially at an end.

Some think the universe will never truly end, instead cycling between big bangs and big crunches on a loop forever.

Chilling effect
Instead of being torn to pieces, all matter may just stop moving.

The Big Crunch

The final idea is the complete opposite—that gravity will in time cause the universe to **stop expanding** and **begin to collapse** in on itself. Everything will crunch together, until all the material in the universe occupies **an infinitely small, hot area**—just like the moment before the Big Bang!

Big Bang → Big Crunch

Crunch... Bang?
It's possible that a Big Crunch could trigger another Big Bang!

No end in sight

Whatever the ultimate **fate of the universe,** you don't really need to worry about it. The earliest anyone thinks the universe might end is **22 billion years into the future**—well past your lifetime, and then some!

WHY STUDY DEEP SPACE?
Studying deep space helps us understand the laws of physics, the age of the universe, and the future of our planet.

Do ALIENS exist?

Life beyond Earth
Since ancient times, people have gazed up at the night sky and wondered if there might be **life out there** somewhere. Could aliens be lurking in our galactic backyard?

Listening out
Radio telescopes on Earth have been listening for alien signals since the 1980s.

Alone in our solar system
Scientists have sent spacecraft to explore our solar system, but so far **no traces of life** have been observed. **Venus and Mars** could have had life billions of years ago. Some scientists think they had **large oceans** just like Earth does now. But today they are **dry, lifeless worlds.**

Venus
If there were oceans on Venus, they have evaporated away, leaving a dry, superhot planet.

Looking farther
Scientists are looking to the **moons of Jupiter and Saturn** as places that might support life, but they are also searching further afield. Thousands of **exoplanets** (planets outside our solar system) have been identified, and more are being discovered all the time. Could it be that a planet **orbiting a distant star** is host to alien life?

HOW WE FIND EXOPLANETS
Scientists use space telescopes to look for new exoplanets. NASA's *TESS* (Transiting Exoplanet Survey Satellite) was launched in 2018 and has found hundreds of them so far. It measures the tiny dip in a star's brightness caused by an exoplanet passing in front of the star.

Watery worlds

Water is the **key to life** on our planet, so this is what scientists are looking for on other planets, too. For **liquid water** to exist, a planet must be in what is called the **habitable zone**—not too close and not too far away from its parent star. Many exoplanets are thought to have water, but they are **so far away** that it hasn't been proven for sure yet.

Stranger things

Of course, this all assumes that life on another planet would be just like life on Earth. If it has **evolved differently,** scientists may simply not know what to look for. Even if we do find signs of life on another planet, **getting there** would be a problem— the closest exoplanet found so far is just under **25 trillion miles (40 trillion km)** away!

Enceladus, a moon of Saturn, has all six of the chemical elements needed for life.

Ice world
Enceladus is covered with ice, but hidden underneath is an ocean where life might exist.

Extreme Earthling
Tiny tardigrades can survive Earth's extremes, showing that life exists in unexpected places.

Out of this world!
Alien life might not be complex and intelligent, but finding microbes on another planet would be just as big a discovery!

WHY LOOK FOR LIFE?
Even if we never find signs of extraterrestrial life, as we find more and more exoplanets, and learn more about them, it shapes our picture of the universe.

Could we ever live on ANOTHER PLANET?

A new home
There may well be planets **similar to Earth** somewhere in the universe, but they are probably so far away that we cannot travel there. As such, if humans ever want to **live on a new planet,** our best bet is to make a nearby planet suitable for humans to live on, using an untested process called **terraforming.**

Engineering an earth
Terraforming is just an idea at the moment, and is **not currently possible.** The most commonly suggested target is Mars—it is just about **within reach of Earth,** but gets much less energy from the sun because it is **farther away.** This makes it cold, not to mention dry and dusty, while its atmosphere contains no oxygen.

Mars
Could the rocky and deserted Martian surface one day bloom with life?

How to terraform
The first step to make a cold, barren planet suitable for humans would be to **warm it up.** Pumping gases such as carbon dioxide into the atmosphere would thicken it, **trapping heat from the sun.** Next we'd have to produce liquid water, and then introduce bacteria and plants. These would help with another hurdle for human life—filling the air with **enough oxygen** for us to breathe.

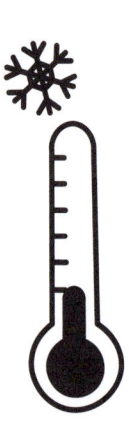

Only 12 people have ever walked on the moon. Nobody else has set foot on land that isn't Earth.

An expensive journey

Delivering all the equipment and resources to terraform Mars seems impossible today—sending even one rocket that far is very **difficult and expensive.** One outlandish idea is to start the process from afar by blasting Mars with **high-powered lasers,** releasing gases from the rocks to form an atmosphere and melting ice to provide water! At present, there are **no practical solutions** even to begin the process.

Starship
Spacecraft like this might one day carry humans to Mars.

SPACE BASE

A few humans already live beyond Earth for months at a time—on space stations orbiting Earth. The first life on another planet will probably be in a protected base like this one.

Space seeds
Astronaut Alexander Gerst displays packs of flower seeds sent into space for a study.

Taking care of our home

Exciting as it is to look for a new home in the stars, we don't know if any of this will work. Perhaps we should focus on **taking care of our own planet!** Humans have caused great damage here, but **it can still be repaired**—and why colonize another world if we have not learned to conserve our own?

Whole Earth
Conserving our world is far less difficult than colonizing a new one.

WHY LIVE ON ANOTHER PLANET?

Even if we can't live full-time on another planet, scientists based there could still learn about the effects of gravity, distance from the sun, and more.

How fast could HUMANS TRAVEL?

No change please

Human bodies don't really like rapid changes. Our bodies are comfortable traveling at high speeds, but can be harmed by a sudden **increase in speed** (acceleration). The fastest a crewed airplane has traveled is **4,520 mph (7,274 km/h)**, but only highly trained pilots can survive a flight like this due to the **extreme acceleration** required to reach this speed.

Don't Stapp!
US Air Force doctor Colonel Stapp experimented with extreme acceleration.

Space pace

In space, there are greater distances to **build up speed** without dangerous acceleration—and far fewer particles of air to slow a craft down. The crew of Apollo 10 reached **25,000 mph (40,000 km/h)** as they returned to Earth from near the moon—the fastest any human has traveled. Scientists say that new engines using **nuclear technology** could in theory propel spacecraft to 500,000 mph (800,000 km/h) or more.

Apollo 10
In 1969, this mission circled the moon before returning to Earth at record speed.

ACCELERATING THE BODY

Extreme acceleration puts severe pressure on the body. It becomes hard to breathe and to pump blood to our brain, so we may even lose vision and fall unconscious until it stops. But don't worry, this only really happens in fighter jets and rockets!

The universal speed limit

But something else in the universe moves **still faster** than this—light! Light particles travel at 671 million mph (1 billion km/h) in a vacuum, and most scientists think it is **impossible to go faster** than this. That's because the faster you travel, the heavier you get, something we don't notice at everyday speeds. Approaching the **speed of light,** you'd become **so heavy** that you could not travel any faster. Case closed?

The International Space Station orbits Earth at 17,501 mph (28,165 km/h).

Light particle
Light is made up of tiny particles called photons. Nothing travels faster!

WHY TRY TO GO FASTER?
The faster we go, the farther we can explore! The journey to Mars takes uncrewed craft about 8 months at present.

Faster than light

Perhaps we don't need to travel faster, just smarter. Imagine that the universe is a large, flat, stretchy sheet of rubber. If you could **pull your destination toward you,** and push your starting point away behind you, you'd arrive almost instantly, an idea called a **"warp drive"**. Or, if this flat sheet could fold in half, you might make a **"wormhole"** to jump to the other half. Is warping space or taking a shortcut even **theoretically possible?** Scientists are a long way from knowing.

Wormhole
If space folds back on itself, perhaps we could make a tunnel to avoid going the long way around.

There may be 2 trillion galaxies in the observable universe alone.

How big is the UNIVERSE?

A bigger ruler

The units we use to measure things on Earth—inches, feet, miles—simply aren't big enough to make sense of **how vast the universe is.** To measure distances in space, scientists use a unit called a **light-year.** This is the distance that light can travel in a year—a colossal 5.88 trillion miles (9.46 trillion km)!

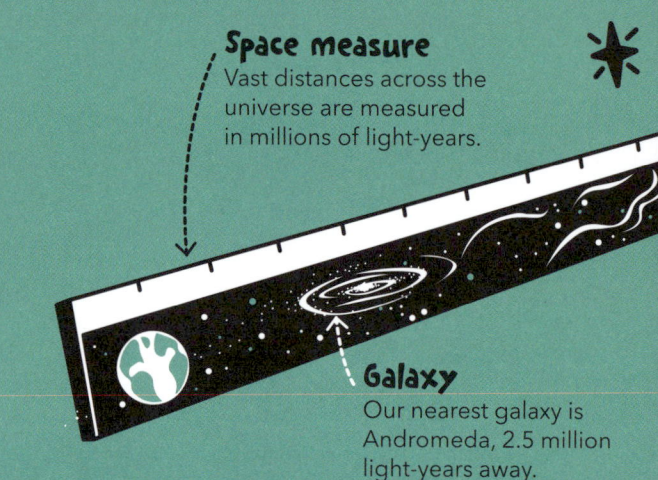

Space measure
Vast distances across the universe are measured in millions of light-years.

Galaxy
Our nearest galaxy is Andromeda, 2.5 million light-years away.

Stretching space

It takes time for light to reach Earth, so the light we see from far away has been traveling for **very long periods of time.** The farthest thing seen so far was a galaxy that existed **13.5 billion years ago,** soon after the universe began. Does that mean it's 13.5 billion light-years away? No! The universe is still expanding, so today that galaxy might be **33 billion light-years** away.

Farthest galaxy
JADES-GS-z14-0 existed just 290 million years after the Big Bang and was full of massive stars.

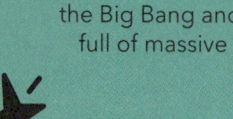

The darkness beyond

The time that light takes to travel, combined with the **expanding universe,** means that light from some stars will **never reach us.** We will only ever be able to see a bubble of space around us—what scientists call the **observable universe.** This is estimated to be about 93 billion light-years wide, but the **actual universe** is much larger.

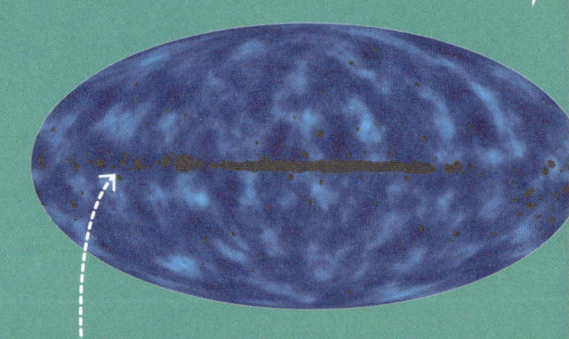

Big bubble
This image depicts the entire observable universe. Brighter areas are superclusters of galaxies. Gray areas are where light from our own galaxy blocks our view.

The hole truth?
The universe could in theory be shaped like a doughnut—but it's unlikely.

How big?!

The whole universe is much bigger than the part we can observe, and is still expanding. It's at least **7 trillion light-years** across, but it might even be **infinitely big,** going on and on forever without an end. Or it may loop back on itself, so that if you travel in a straight line, you will eventually end up **back where you started!**

THE JAMES WEBB SPACE TELESCOPE

On Earth, the atmosphere blurs our view, so scientists put special telescopes in space to see farther. The James Webb Space Telescope, launched in 2021, has given us our deepest view ever into the distant universe.

WHY STUDY THE SIZE OF THE UNIVERSE?
Studying the size of the universe helps us understand how it began, what is happening now, and what might happen in the future.

Mirror
The main mirror, 21 ft (6.5 m) wide, collects light from distant stars.

Instruments
Special sensors beam data back to Earth.

Zoom lens
A telescope helps us to see farther into the night sky.

Why does GRAVITY EXIST?

Black holes have such strong gravity that they can even pull in light—which is why they appear black, because no light can escape from them.

Feeling the pull

Gravity is an invisible force that **pulls objects together**—when you jump upward, it pulls you back to Earth. Mass is the **amount of matter** in an object, and matter is what makes up the universe we see around us. Gravity acts between **any two objects that have mass,** but we only notice it with really massive objects such as planets and stars.

Leap here
You could jump less than half as high on Jupiter as you can on Earth.

Unknown pressures

The more mass an object has, the stronger its gravitational pull. Gravity on the surface of the massive planet Jupiter, for example, is **2.5 times stronger** than on Earth. The pull of gravity keeps the moon orbiting the Earth, planets circling our sun, and our galaxy spinning around its center. It's clear that **gravity holds the universe together,** but scientists don't fully understand how it works—**or why it exists** in the first place!

Sir Isaac Newton
The story goes that an apple falling on this famous scientist's head inspired his theory of gravity!

Jupiter
This giant planet has 318 times the mass of Earth.

GRAVITY AND ORBITS

If gravity pulls objects together, then why do planets orbit the sun, or satellites circle the Earth without falling down? This is because their forward speed matches the downward pull of gravity.

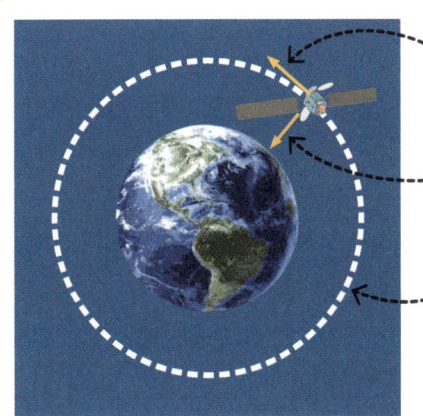

Velocity
Without other forces, the satellite would continue in a straight line.

Gravity
This pulls the satellite toward Earth.

Circular orbit
The combination of forces results in a circular path.

Bending space

Imagine our universe is a **flat sheet** of stretchy material. If you put something massive on top, say a bowling ball, it will cause **a dip in the sheet.** Place something much less massive nearby, like a pea, and it will roll toward the bowling ball, like an object **falling to Earth.** Roll the pea fast past the bowling ball, and it will move in a curve, like an orbiting satellite. This is how some scientists suggest gravity works, by **bending and distorting** space itself!

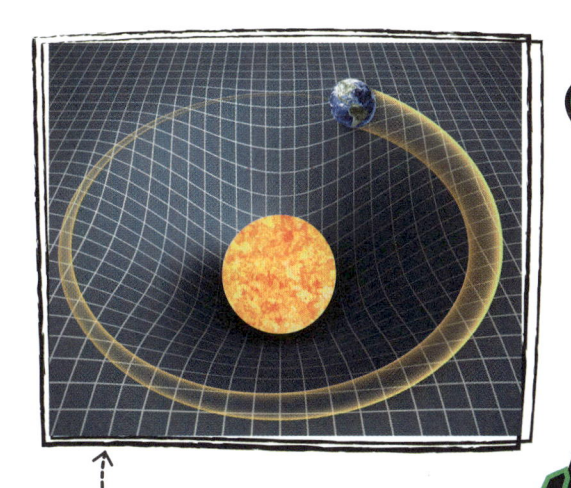

Mind-bending
What if Earth is flying straight, but space itself is curved?

The mystery particle

Many scientists also believe that gravity may be caused by a **mysterious tiny particle,** just as light is caused by particles called photons. They have named this particle the **graviton,** but it has not yet been detected. If found, it will help solve one of science's **biggest mysteries** about how the universe works.

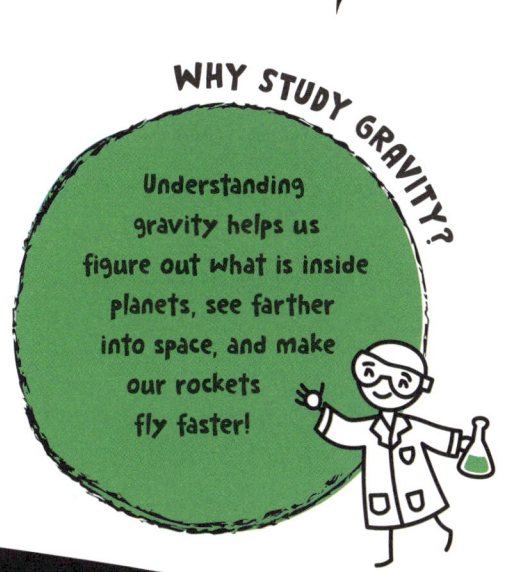

WHY STUDY GRAVITY?
Understanding gravity helps us figure out what is inside planets, see farther into space, and make our rockets fly faster!

HOW DID THE MOON FORM?

Violent beginnings

The early years of our solar system were **chaotic and violent.** After the sun formed, a vast flat cloud of rocks, gases, and dust were left **spinning around it.** Within this mess, gravity started to pull things together, forming larger rocky objects. These crashed into each other again and again, **clumping together** to form the planets we see today.

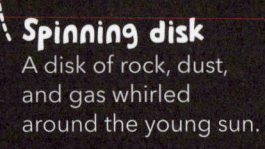

Spinning disk
A disk of rock, dust, and gas whirled around the young sun.

Adopted asteroid or rocky twin?

For a long time, scientists thought the moon had been a **large space rock** called an asteroid, which drifted close to Earth and was **pulled into orbit** by gravity. The astronauts who walked on the moon in the 1960s and 1970s brought **pieces of moon rock** back to test this idea. Scientists were amazed to find **similarities with rocks found on Earth**—could the moon have formed at the same time as Earth, from the same cloud of dust?

Nearside
We only ever see one side of the moon from Earth!

The moon is moving away from Earth at a rate of 1.5 in (3.8 cm) every year—about the same speed your fingernails grow!

50

Lunar sea
The darker patches of rock on the moon, called seas, were once lakes of lava.

HOW THE MOON AFFECTS EARTH

The moon's gravity pulls water on Earth toward it, causing a high tide where oceans meet land. As Earth turns, the part nearest the moon changes, so different places experience high and low tides in turn.

Far side
Earth's rotation forms a second high tide on the far side from the Moon.

High tide
The Moon's gravity pulls water towards it.

Collisions and chaos

Or perhaps a giant object the size of Mars **crashed into Earth,** throwing up a cloud of debris that in time became the moon? This theoretical **giant object, named Theia,** would have left a lot of material on Earth, with the rest forming the moon—this would explain why rocks from both are similar. Scientists have also found **huge lumps of metal** deep inside Earth, which may have been Theia's core.

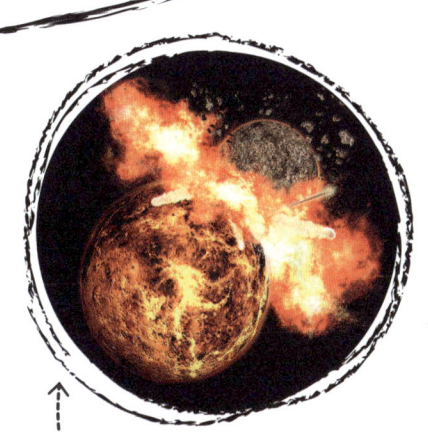

Cosmic collision
A lump of space rock the size of Mars may have collided with Earth.

Searching for evidence

Most scientists now think the moon was formed by a massive collision, but **more evidence is needed.** We have only a small amount of moon rock to study—880 lbs (about 400 kg) or **three wheelbarrows full**—from a handful of sites. Only by collecting more samples and peering **deeper into our own planet** can we be sure about the origin of our moon.

WHY STUDY THE MOON?

The moon is our closest neighbor, full of clues to Earth's deep history and how the solar system formed.

Why do we AGE?

Smile!
Studies suggest that a positive attitude may extend your life.

An age-old mystery

We spend about 20 years growing up, getting ready to take on the world, yet **the moment we reach adulthood** we begin to age. Our bodies become a little less flexible and injuries take longer to heal. **From 30, we start to shrink a tiny bit,** and by 40 our speed and strength are past their peak. As decades pass, our hair grays, skin wrinkles, bones weaken, and eventually our bodies stop working. **This is a natural part of life,** but scientists don't know exactly why it happens.

Nucleus

Aging cell
Individual cells in our bodies get damaged over time, die, and are replaced.

The damage adds up

Aging involves a slow buildup of damage to the cells that make up your body. **Many things in the environment** can damage us—radiation from the sun, the food you eat, the air you breathe, illness, or even prolonged stress. Your body repairs **most, but not all,** of the damage, so it **builds up over time.** Could we protect ourselves and live longer?

Community spirit
A thriving social life seems to help people live longer.

Some parts of Japan, Italy, Greece, Costa Rica, and the US seem to have more long-lived people than others. Different scientists put this down to local diet, climate, social structure, genetics, or even record-keeping mistakes!

THE SECRET TO LONGER LIFE?

52

Change is inevitable

Scientists think our bodies likely have **a built-in lifespan,** and that we would age even if we avoided all external damage to our cells and bodies. Healthy habits may extend this lifespan, but **at a certain point** even the best-protected body will stop working. Your lifespan may be coded into the DNA you inherited from your parents, which makes sense as **siblings of people who live to 100** are also more likely to live to an old age.

Turning back the clock

We may not know exactly why we age, but some scientists are trying to **slow or even reverse** the process. They study foods, lifestyles, and drugs that may help us **live longer, healthier lives,** and examine the DNA of people and animals that age more slowly. So far, nobody has lived past 122, but perhaps **the first person to live to 150** has already been born!

DN-Age
Our DNA may have a built-in age limit that stops us living forever.

WHY STUDY AGING?
Humans have always dreamed of eternal youth. More realistically, research into aging can help us to live healthier, happier, and longer lives.

Growing, pains
As soon as we stop growing, we start to age.

Shrinking feeling
In old age, we become a little shorter and weaker.

Why do we LAUGH?

No joke
Babies seem to chuckle before they even understand what they are laughing at.

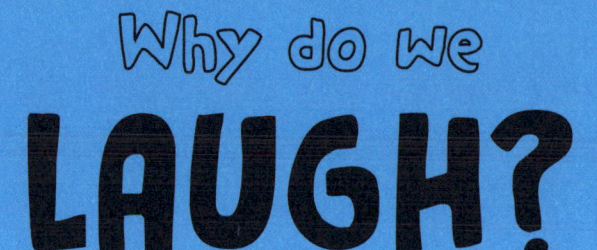

Laughter is everywhere
Anywhere you visit in the world, no matter what age people are or what language they speak, you will hear laughter. **We start laughing as babies,** before we've even learned to talk. And it isn't just humans—our close relatives **chimpanzees and orangutans** laugh too, with a loud hooting sound, and even **tickle each other** when playing! But what are we all laughing for?

The oldest recorded joke is about farting! It dates back to 1900 BCE.

Keeping company
You are many times more likely to laugh simply if someone else is there. Scientists therefore think that laughter is **an important signal** to others. Most of the time we are not laughing at a particular joke, but a situation or event. **Social laughter** avoids awkwardness, showing others that you are friendly and **not a threat,** and even that you agree with them.

Fall in laugh
When you laugh really hard, it can be difficult to stay upright.

Making friends

Chimpanzees and other apes spend time **cleaning each other's fur** and removing insects. This is called grooming and it helps them to **build friendships.** Laughter might be a way for us to do the same thing in our larger social groups—**laughing together** builds bonds and shows our friends that we like them and enjoy spending time together.

Nitpicking
Chimpanzees bond by combing their friends' fur for dirt, plants, dried skin, and bugs.

WHAT IS LAUGHTER?

When we laugh, our lungs pull in big breaths of air and push them out again in waves, making us go, "Ha, ha, ha." Muscles in the face pull our mouths wider, and our shoulders may shake up and down. Real laughter is involuntary—we don't decide to do it; it just happens.

WHY STUDY LAUGHTER?

Laughing makes us feel so good that scientists are studying whether they could use it alongside medicine!

A good laugh
Laughing releases chemicals called endorphins, which make you feel better.

The best medicine

It could be that we laugh simply because it is **good for our health!** Laughing encourages us to breathe deeply, increasing the supply of oxygen to our internal organs and keeping them healthy. Laughing also **reduces stress,** floods the brain with chemicals that make us happy, and even **exercises some of our muscles.** So whatever the reason we laugh, keep it up to stay happy and healthy!

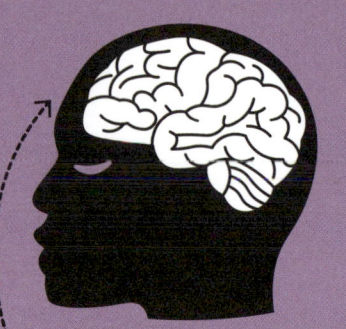

Why do we DREAM?

Headquarters
The brain sits in the top half of our head, protected by the bony skull.

Busy brain

At night, your brain cycles between **two types of behavior.** The first is **deep sleep**. This is what we imagine when we think of sleep, with steady regular breathing and little movement. **Lighter sleep,** however, is **quite different**—your heartbeat races, your eyes flicker, and your brain uses as much energy as when you are awake. Lighter sleep is **when you have dreams.**

Mostly meaningless

Our dreams can be **strange, exciting, or scary,** but what are they for? Some scientists think that **dreams mean nothing** at all. It could be that what we experience as dreams are simply caused by your **brain randomly activating** while you are asleep.

Sleeping duty
Adults need 7-9 hours of sleep per night, but children's developing brains need 9-12.

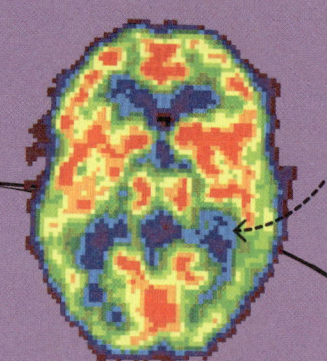

WHEN WHAT HAPPENS YOU DREAM

Awake — Deep sleep — Dreaming

Quiet zone
Blue areas are the least active.

These brain scans show which parts of the brain are active at different times, with red areas the busiest. They clearly show that your brain doesn't switch off when you sleep—in fact, some parts can be more active while dreaming than when awake! Scientists think it is busy processing your memories and emotions of the day.

Flying high
In our dreams, we can do the impossible.

Nightmares might be good for you! Scientists think they help us tackle our fears so that we are less afraid in real life.

Building memories

On the other hand, dreams could be how we store our memories. Dreaming helps us to go through **what we have seen during the day,** and remember the things that seem important. It may also **strengthen memories** of the past by recalling them as we sleep.

Learning and growing

Dreaming might also give us the chance to learn from our experiences. As we dream, we are **reliving the emotions** we experienced during the day. This could help us to **process what we have gone through** in a safe environment, helping us to be more resilient in the future.

Electric dreams
Sleep scientists use sensors to monitor patients' brainwaves while they sleep.

It came to me in a dream

Another reason to dream could be to make us more creative! Dreams help **our minds wander freely,** without the rest of life getting in the way. Many artists say that their best ideas come to them in their sleep. So make sure you **keep paper and pencil by your bed,** just in case inspiration strikes in your dreams!

WHY STUDY DREAMS?
Studying why we dream helps scientists understand how our brains work overall. This can help them treat problems that happen in the brain.

Why do we YAWN?

Finding the answers

Yawning might seem to be a very simple behavior—we yawn when **we're tired,** right? But **we don't yawn every time** we're sleepy, and sometimes we yawn when we're not tired at all! Scientists don't know **exactly why we yawn,** but they have lots of ideas. It's possible that more than one of these is correct.

Early yawning
All humans yawn, from young babies to old people. Even babies in the womb have been seen yawning!

The wrong idea

There is, however, one popular idea that scientists have **shown to be unlikely.** For a long time, people thought that yawning was a way to bring **more oxygen into the body** when needed. But when scientists tested this by reducing the amount of oxygen in the air of a room, **people did not yawn more,** suggesting that this theory is incorrect.

ANATOMY OF A YAWN

Yawning draws in a big breath of air, opening our airways as wide as possible by contracting some muscles and relaxing others. A typical yawn lasts 4–7 seconds and they often come in threes, each larger than the one before.

Wide open
When we yawn, the muscles marked red contract and those in blue are stretched.

You are more likely to "catch" a yawn from someone nearby if they are a friend or family member than if they are a total stranger.

Infectious yawn
Looking at this picture might make you yawn, too! When others yawn, so do we.

Time to wake up

People often yawn when they are **feeling bored or tired.** Rather than being something caused by feeling sleepy, some scientists suggest yawning is an automatic process **to tackle tiredness!** Yawning activates lots of muscles, increasing your heart rate and **waking you up,** if only for a small period of time.

Cooling down

Some scientists think we might **yawn to cool down.** As you yawn, you increase the flow of blood near the surface of your face and **expose the inside of your mouth** to the open air. This allows the blood to **lose heat more easily,** cooling it down and lowering your temperature.

Air conditioning
Letting all that air into its mouth may help this tiger cool its brain from below.

Yawning hello

Have you ever felt the **urge to yawn** when someone else does? You're not alone. Humans are one of the **most social animals,** and so scientists think this is another way we communicate. When people yawn, **we often copy them,** which shows that we understand what they are feeling. But don't start **yawning hello** next time you meet a friend—it can signal boredom, too!

WHY STUDY YAWNING?

Almost all animals with a backbone yawn—from cats and crocodiles to birds and fish—so it clearly has at least one important purpose.

Why do we get HICCUPS?

Hic!

Unwanted surprises

We all know the dreaded feeling: out of nowhere, a sudden jerk in your tummy, **an uncontrollable "HIC!"** in your throat, and the nervous wait for the next jerk. Why are you hiccupping, and **when will it stop?** We're not entirely sure, but we know this happens more to children than adults, and **can also affect animals** including pandas, squirrels, dogs, and cats!

WHAT IS A HICCUP?

Your diaphragm is a stretchy sheet of muscle under your lungs. Usually, this pulls down smoothly to draw air into your lungs, but sometimes it starts to jerk unpredictably.

Air in

Hic!
A sudden gulp of air makes a flap in your throat called the epiglottis snap shut with a loud "hic!"

Diaphragm

Lung

A man in the United States had hiccups continuously for 68 years—the world record. They only stopped when he was 96!

Quirky cure
Drinking from the "wrong" side of the glass might make you focus so hard that your brain "forgets" to hiccup!

WHY STUDY HICCUPS?

Scientists want to understand why nerves misfire, how this affects our health, and how we can reset them to make us better.

Goodbye gas

There are many ideas for why we might hiccup. One likely purpose is to **get rid of air from our stomachs.** When drinking milk, babies can swallow air by accident. Hiccups help release this air, and are also seen in **other baby animals that drink milk,** like kittens and puppies. Adults may need to get rid of air trapped in their stomach, either from carbonated drinks or **eating too fast.**

Losing control

Some scientists suggest hiccups happen when we are nervous, excited, or stressed. **The vagus nerve,** which carries messages from our brain to our diaphragm, gut, and more, may play a role—it can be triggered by **stress, indigestion, or even a stray hair** tickling your eardrum. When overstimulated, the nerve might deliver **a faulty signal** to your diaphragm, causing hiccups.

Hic-causes
Eating and drinking too fast could bring on a bout of hiccups.

The missing cure

Since we don't know exactly why we get hiccups, it's hardly surprising that there is **no proven cure.** People have tried lots of remedies, some stranger than others—**gargling ice-cold water** or biting into a lemon, **pulling on their tongue,** breathing through a straw, or even holding their breath, sometimes while spinning around! Thankfully, most hiccups will **simply stop** after a while without drastic measures.

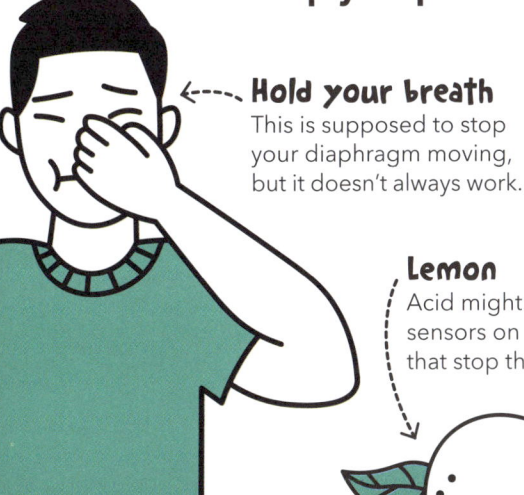

Hold your breath
This is supposed to stop your diaphragm moving, but it doesn't always work.

Ice water
Drinking very cold water might help halt hiccups.

Shock treatment
A sudden surprise might stop hiccups— or start them!

Lemon
Acid might trigger sensors on your tongue that stop the hiccups.

Why do we have FINGERPRINTS?

Uniquely yours

Your fingerprints—the **patterns of texture** on your **fingertips**—are completely unique to you. Just like the stripes on a zebra, or the spots on a cheetah, their arrangement is **completely random.** They developed as you were growing in the womb, and **will barely change** throughout your life. But why do we have them at all? There are **competing theories** as to why they first developed.

Spot check
The pattern of spots on a leopard is as unique as a fingerprint.

Monkeying around

Our closest animal ancestors, the great apes, **have fingerprints too.** This led scientists to think we might all have them for **the same reason**—to help us swing through the jungle. Perhaps the ridges give us **better grip** on rough surfaces to avoid untimely slips, or maybe they **flex like rubber** to protect our fingers from painful blisters?

Island
A short ridge with no connections is called an island.

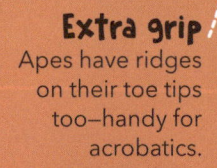

Extra grip
Apes have ridges on their toe tips too—handy for acrobatics.

Koalas have fingerprints that are remarkably similar to humans—bad news if they commit a crime!

Ridge ending
Noting where ridges begin and end helps to identify prints.

Fork
A fork is where one line divides into two.

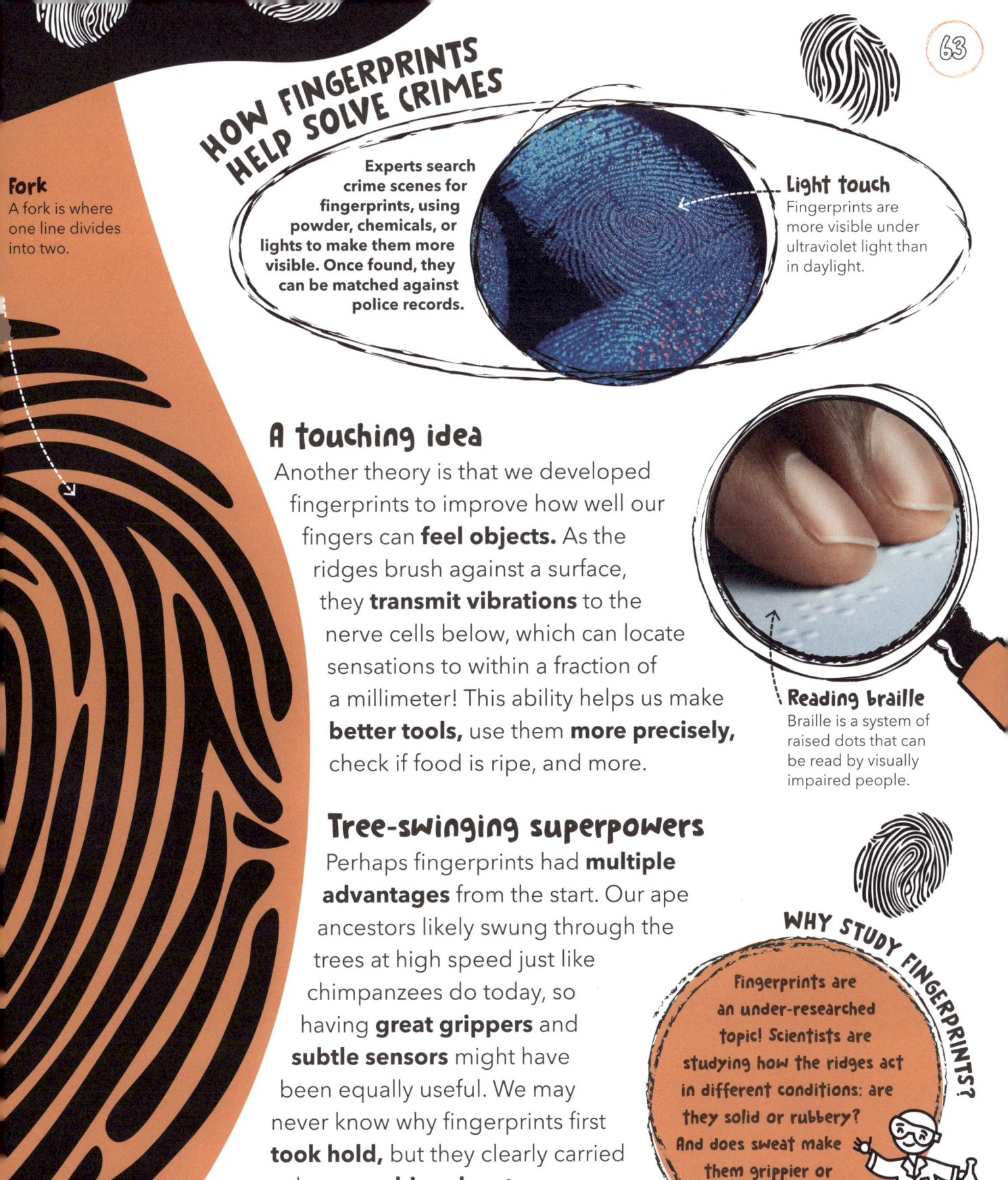

HOW FINGERPRINTS HELP SOLVE CRIMES

Experts search crime scenes for fingerprints, using powder, chemicals, or lights to make them more visible. Once found, they can be matched against police records.

Light touch
Fingerprints are more visible under ultraviolet light than in daylight.

A touching idea

Another theory is that we developed fingerprints to improve how well our fingers can **feel objects.** As the ridges brush against a surface, they **transmit vibrations** to the nerve cells below, which can locate sensations to within a fraction of a millimeter! This ability helps us make **better tools,** use them **more precisely,** check if food is ripe, and more.

Reading braille
Braille is a system of raised dots that can be read by visually impaired people.

Tree-swinging superpowers

Perhaps fingerprints had **multiple advantages** from the start. Our ape ancestors likely swung through the trees at high speed just like chimpanzees do today, so having **great grippers** and **subtle sensors** might have been equally useful. We may never know why fingerprints first **took hold,** but they clearly carried at least one **big advantage.**

WHY STUDY FINGERPRINTS?

Fingerprints are an under-researched topic! Scientists are studying how the ridges act in different conditions: are they solid or rubbery? And does sweat make them grippier or more slippery?

Why do we have an APPENDIX?

A pain in the guts

Your appendix is a **small, wormlike tube** about the length of a finger, jutting off your intestine in the lower **right-hand side of your tummy.** You probably haven't thought about your appendix much in your life. Most people only pay attention if it **starts to hurt** and they have to see a doctor for help—and if someone has their appendix removed, they can do **just fine without it.**

The longest human appendix on record was a whopping 10 in (26 cm) long—almost triple the usual length!

Large intestine
This part of the gut turns digested food into poop.

Ouch!
When the appendix gets infected, it may have to be removed quickly.

WHERE OUR FOOD GOES

- Small intestine
- Large intestine
- Appendix
- Stomach

During digestion, food is broken down in the mouth and stomach; then it passes into the small intestine, which absorbs nutrients. The remains enter the large intestine, passing the entrance to the appendix, and eventually exit the body as poop.

Appendicitis
If a small piece of partly digested food gets stuck in this dead end, the appendix swells painfully.

Just hanging around

For a long time, many scientists thought the human appendix did **nothing at all** and was left over from our evolutionary past. The appendix is much larger in animals that eat only raw plants, and it appears to help them to **digest tough material,** such as tree bark and grass fibers. Early human ancestors ate foods like this, so perhaps our appendix **was once useful.** As we started to hunt and cook, our diet changed and so, the theory went, this part slowly shrank.

Long appendix
A koala's appendix can be 6.5 ft (2 m) long! It helps them digest eucalyptus leaves.

Appendix army
The appendix stores and produces immune cells that fight disease.

Lying in wait

However, recent research suggests that the human appendix **might not be so useless** after all. Scientists have discovered that it is actually **packed full of immune cells**—the special defense cells your body makes to fight off infections. It could be that the appendix holds an army of cells, **ready to attack any infections** in your gut.

Home for microscopic friends

And it is not just human cells that live in your appendix. Your gut is full of **friendly bacteria,** which help you digest food and keep you healthy. Scientists now think that your appendix might store these friendly bacteria, so that if you are sick and **bacteria die off** in your gut, this reserve can quickly multiply and **help again.** Whatever its precise role, it seems your appendix is not just hanging around doing nothing!

WHY STUDY THE APPENDIX?
Up to 10 percent of people have appendicitis at some point in their lives, so it's worth knowing what the appendix does!

How do BICYCLES stay upright?

A confusing ride

The design of bicycles today is **fairly similar** to those first invented **over 200 years ago,** but the humble two-wheeler is still a puzzle to scientists. Why does it fall over when stationary, but **stay upright when moving?**

A moving problem

One common explanation is the **gyroscopic effect**—the same reason that a spinning Frisbee flies straight, or a coin rolls along a table. Once a **heavy disk** such as your bike wheel **starts to spin,** it doesn't easily tilt or fall over until it slows down. But this **doesn't have much effect** until a bike is traveling faster than the average adult cycles, so it can't be the main reason.

No hands!
Even the simple bicycles of the 1890s could stay upright when moving without much help.

There are thought to be more than 1 billion bicycles in the world. Half of them are the Chinese-made "Flying Pigeon".

Wheel speed
Racing bike wheels have some gyroscopic effect when spinning fast.

THE INSIDE ANGLE ON BICYCLE DESIGN

Bicycle makers look at every angle, surface, and part to make the machine work better. For example, a longer bicycle may be more stable, but a shorter one will respond faster to steering.

Fork path
The angle at which the fork meets the front wheel hub affects stability and steering.

Stable bolter
A bicycle rolling downhill can stay upright for a surprisingly long way.

Driverless bicycles

Perhaps it is **mainly the rider** that makes a bike stable? When a bike starts to lean, the front wheel **must turn to the same side** to bring the bike back upright. You do this every few seconds without even thinking about it. Yet many bikes can **roll along without a rider**—push one at a good speed or point it downhill and the bike will keep going until it slows down. If it tilts to one side, it can even **regain its balance!**

WHY STUDY BICYCLES?

Understanding the balancing forces at work can help us to build faster and safer bikes.

Weighting game

Scientists have found that if there is enough weight at the **front of the bike,** the front wheel will turn to the side without human help, **steering the bike back** into a stable position. Is this the answer? Not exactly—scientists have also built stable bikes **without weight on the front wheel!** While they keep puzzling over how different effects combine and searching for a magic formula, let's just be thankful for the **mysterious balance** of bicycles.

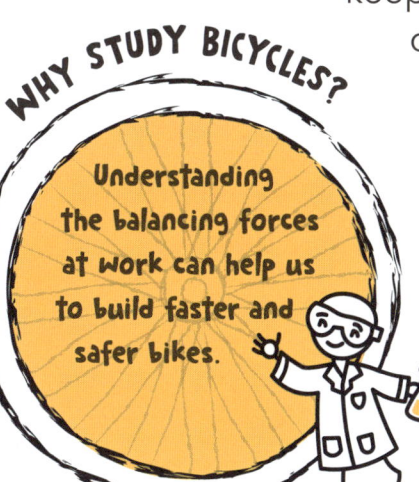

How do airplanes STAY IN THE AIR?

Winging it

If you've ever sat in an airplane for **takeoff,** almost deafened by the noise, you'd be forgiven for thinking that **powerful engines** are the key to keeping a plane in the air. The engines, however, simply keep the aircraft moving fast—**the secret to flight lies in the wings.** There are two main explanations for how airplanes stay in the air, but neither quite explains everything!

Jet set
Modern jet aircraft have one set of wings and two or four engines.

Under pressure

Many airplane wings have **the same basic shape**—a flat bottom and a slightly domed top side. The shape makes air **flow faster** over the top of the wing than the bottom, which causes **lower pressure** above the wing than below it. We don't know why this happens, but it **pushes the wings upward** as they travel through the air. Problem solved, almost! But how do stunt aircraft fly upside down?

Daredevils
Stunt planes can fly upside down if the pilot keeps their wings at the right angle.

Balancing forces

This is where the other explanation comes into play. As an airplane travels through the sky, it is **constantly bombarded** by particles of air in its path. So long as the wing of an airplane is **angled just right,** the force of these air molecules pushing against the underside of the wing **lifts the plane** higher into the sky.

Plane sailing
Paper planes still glide even without curved wing surfaces. They rely on the angle of the wings to keep them aloft.

68

Speedy spinner
Propellers work by hurling a mass of air backward, causing the plane to move forward.

Wings are not just for planes—race cars use upside down wings to push them downward, so they grip the track better!

Winging it
A biplane has two main wings stacked one above the other.

HOW WINGS WORK

Because an airplane's wing is curved, air traveling across the top surface ends up traveling faster than the air along the bottom surface. This causes lower pressure above the wing than below it, which results in lift.

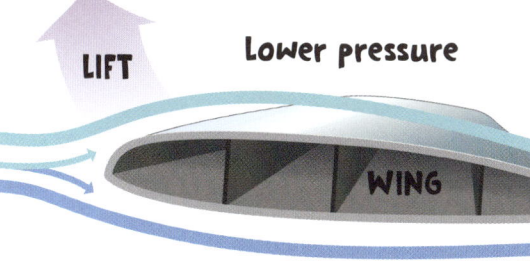

LIFT
Lower pressure
WING
Higher pressure

Flying together

So which of these two explanations is actually correct? Experts think it might be **both of them.** It's even possible that each makes the other work better, together resulting in **nice stable flight.** So no need to worry next time you hop on a plane!

WHY STUDY PLANES?

Scientists study aerodynamics to design faster, safer, and more efficient aircraft. New designs save fuel and cause less damage to the environment.

Could TIME TRAVEL become a reality?

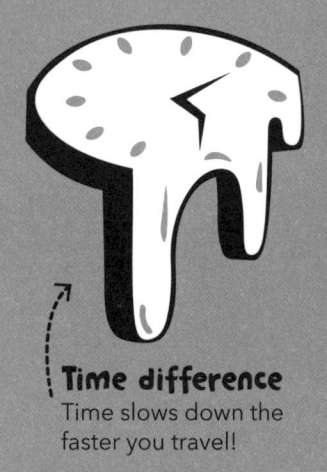

What is time travel?
In a way, **we are all time travelers.** We are moving forward through time into the future, moment by moment, year after year. But because we move into the future **at the same rate** as everyone around us, it **feels normal.** When we talk about time travel, we usually mean the ability to move through time **in a different way** than everyone else.

Time difference
Time slows down the faster you travel!

Joining space and time
To understand how the universe works, scientists think of **space and time together.** By joining the three dimensions of space (left/right, forward/backward, and up/down) with time, scientists talk about **four-dimensional "space-time".** In this theory, the flow of time isn't constant, but can change under different conditions.

Time machine
For now, time machines exist only in science fiction and our imaginations.

In 2009, British scientist Stephen Hawking hosted a party for time travelers, but he only sent out invitations the day after the party. No one turned up!

70

TIME TRAVELER

Astronaut Scott Kelly spent a year on the International Space Station, which travels at more than 17,500 mph (28,000 km/h). At this speed, less time passed for him than for us on Earth, so he returned an extra 13 milliseconds younger than his identical twin brother!

Racing into the future

Scientists have found that **the faster you travel, the more slowly time passes** for you compared to someone standing still. If you were to travel very fast in space for a year, **more time would pass on Earth** than on your spaceship—so when you returned to Earth, you would arrive **more than one Earth year** into the future! However, for this to be noticeable, you would have to travel at close to the speed of light.

Finding a way back

If going forward in time is hard, then traveling to the past may be impossible without **altering space-time itself.** One mind-bending idea is to make a "time doughnut" by folding space-time together to **connect the past and the future.** Another idea is to form a long string of rapidly wiggling **"space spaghetti"** 10 times heavier than our sun. Flying around this would send you back in time—but the extreme gravity would also **crush your spaceship** to dust!

Space spaghetti
Theoretically, space-time itself could be bent and squeezed.

Where are the visitors?

If time travel to the past might one day be possible, why aren't we being visited by **time-traveling humans** from the far distant future? Some scientists think this tells us that **backward time travel** will never be possible, whatever creative ideas we think up to explain how it could happen!

WHY STUDY TIME TRAVEL?

Time "travel" already affects us—satellites orbiting the planet at high speeds have to have their clocks adjusted to stay synchronized with us on Earth!

Can we keep making faster COMPUTERS?

Slow computers

Early modern computers, built in the 1940s, were **colossal machines** that filled entire rooms and took hours to perform simple calculations. Since then, computer engineers have made them **ever smaller and faster,** performing more and more calculations per second. Can they keep doing this, or **is there a limit** to how powerful computers can be?

Early computer
The Electronic Numerical Integrator and Computer (ENIAC), built in 1945, was the size of a room.

CHIPS WITH EVERYTHING

In a computer, tiny transistors are packed together on thin wafers of silicon called chips. These link the transistors in circuits to control complex tasks (logic chips) or store information (memory chips).

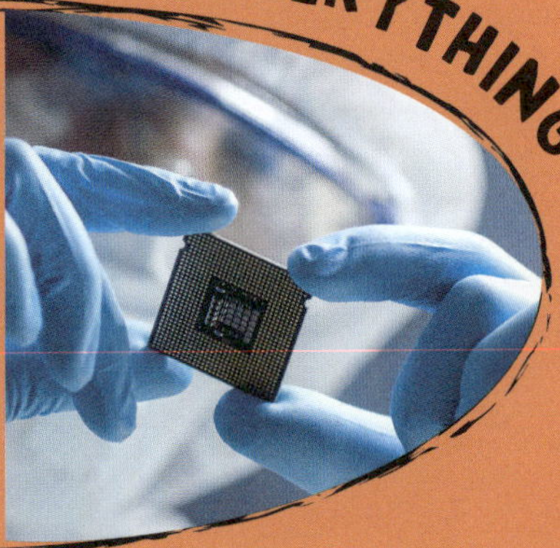

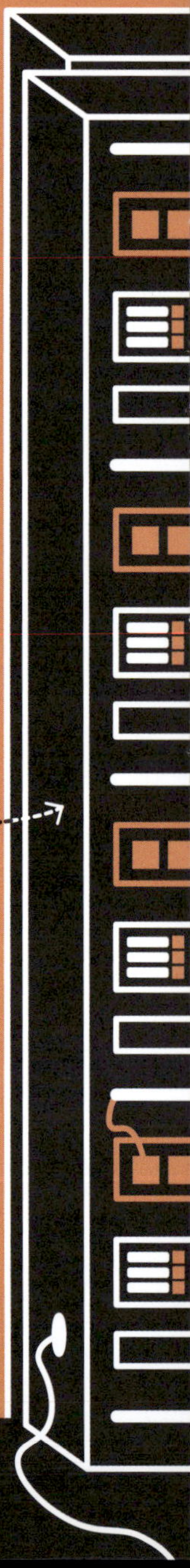

"The cloud"
Today, most of our processing takes place in vast data centers.

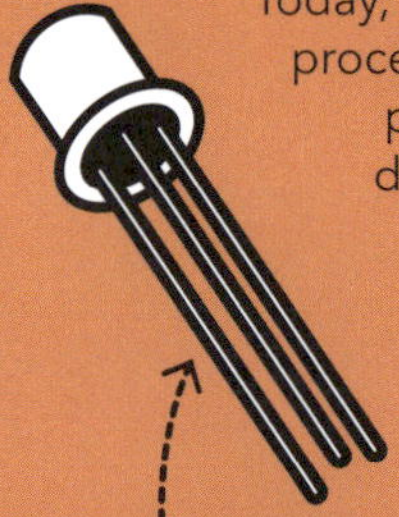

Early transistor
Today's transistors are too small to see.

It's all in the switches

Most computers today work in much the same way as those early machines. They contain little **electrical switches called transistors.** These turn on and off billions of times per second, allowing a computer to make calculations. **Making them smaller** not only lets you fit more into a given space, but also makes them **operate faster** and use **less energy.** In general, the more transistors your computer has, the more powerful it will be.

An average mobile phone today is more than one million times more powerful than the computer that helped land humans on the moon in 1969.

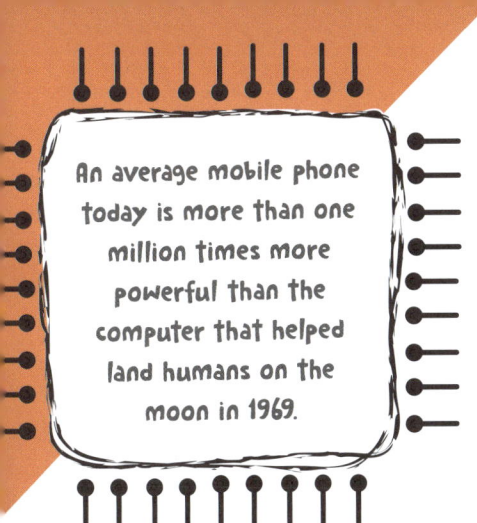

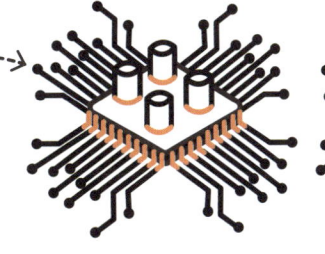

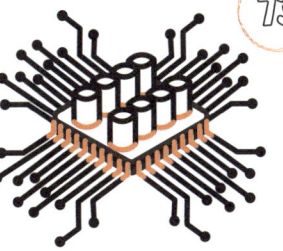

Double power
From 4 transistors to 8 is a small step, but 17 more doublings take us past one million.

Shrinking down

The number of transistors in a new computer roughly **doubles every two years,** making them faster and faster. This is only possible because scientists are **shrinking transistors** to microscopic sizes. Where the first transistors were about 0.4 in (1 cm) across, today hundreds of billions fit on a fingertip. But we might be close to hitting **physical limits**—some transistor parts simply can't be smaller than a single atom.

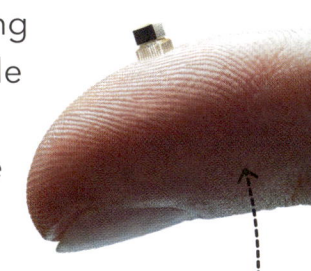

Microprocessor
These powerful chips contain billions of tiny transistors.

Diving into uncertainty

To keep up the rate of progress, scientists are exploring new approaches. One of these is **quantum computing.** In most electronics, a transistor can either be on or off, which a computer reads as 1 or 0. A quantum transistor, however, can be both **1 and 0 at the same time!** This makes quantum computers **millions of times faster** than a normal machine, but only for certain tasks, and only when kept incredibly cold. If the next generation of processors **cannot be used at home,** we may instead link our personal computers to ever more powerful ones in data centers.

Smart phone
Our devices connect to more powerful processors via the internet.

WHY STUDY MICROPROCESSORS?
Ever-smaller microprocessors have already enabled space travel, smartphones, and artificial intelligence. Who knows what the next decade will bring?

Will computers become SMARTER THAN HUMANS?

Following instructions
Modern computers are super-powerful and can perform **trillions of calculations** per second. They already affect every aspect of our lives, from **predicting the weather** to making special effects for movies, and can **beat humans at chess** and other games. No matter how powerful they are, though, most computers are still just **following instructions** given to them by humans.

More than 75 percent of companies around the world already use some form of artificial intelligence.

Bionic brain
Some scientists think we could one day merge HI (human intelligence) with AI.

A thinking computer
The technology to allow a computer to think for itself is called **artificial intelligence** or **AI**. Scientists have been exploring this for as long as computers have existed, but had to wait until computers were more powerful for AI to progress rapidly. To make **a computer that can think for itself,** scientists are writing computer programs that learn to take in information, **look for patterns,** and make decisions.

Brain scan
Computers can compare one scan with another to spot changes.

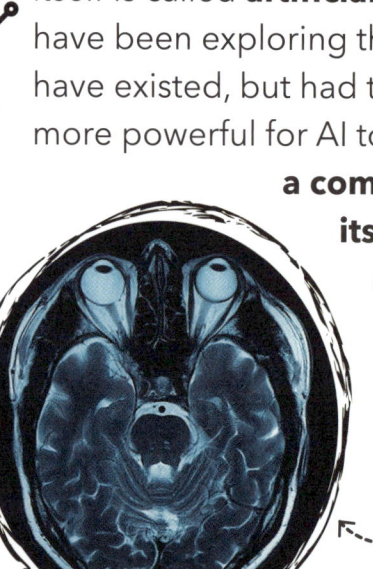

74

Not quite human

Today, a new type of AI, called **generative AI,** can perform some creative tasks a bit like humans do, such as writing or drawing. It does this by taking in a large library of data (e.g. one billion webpages), looking through it for **patterns and similarities,** and using this to create "new" work. This may be useful for research, but also **makes mistakes.** Scientists don't consider AI like this to be smarter than humans, because anything it creates is basically a **remix of existing work** made by humans.

Not so smart
AI images often have errors, such as the extra tails on this cat.

ALL TOO HUMAN

Most AI exists in computers, but scientists are trying to make "embodied AI"–robots that look like us and can do human tasks. These would be useful, but could also make dangerous mistakes. And some people think that if AI becomes too smart, it will replace us all.

Human form
A robot in human shape is called a humanoid robot.

The everything machine

The ultimate aim for some scientists is to design **artificial general intelligence**—AI that is flexible enough to tackle any mental task, not just answer a specific question. Humans use **imagination, creativity, and problem-solving** even for simple tasks such as loading a dishwasher. These are all skills that computers find very difficult, so it will take **a lot more time** to make a computer smarter than humans—and it may not be desirable or possible at all!

WHY STUDY AI?

AI can do some tasks much faster than humans. Ideally, it will give us more time for interesting work and having fun!

GLOSSARY

Acceleration
A change in speed—the rate at which an object's speed changes.

Artificial intelligence (AI)
Computer systems designed to think and learn so they can do tasks that would normally require human intelligence.

Asteroid
A rocky object smaller than a planet but larger than 3.3 ft (1 m) across that orbits the sun.

Backbone
A column of bones running down the center of an animal's back that provides support for the body.

Bacteria
Tiny, single-celled lifeforms. A few of these cause diseases in humans.

Cell
The basic unit that makes up all plants and animals, containing instructions, liquid, and a cell membrane to hold it all together.

Computer chip
A set of electronic circuits on a small, flat piece of silicon. A computer works by switching these circuits on and off very fast.

Crustacean
An animal with a hard external shell, two pairs of antennae and several pairs of jointed legs, such as a crab, shrimp, or lobster.

Cycad
A tropical evergreen plant that looks like a short, sturdy palm tree. They were common millions of years ago but are rarer today.

Dark energy
A type of energy that scientists cannot currently detect, but think must exist based on how objects in the universe are behaving.

Data center
A large group of linked computers that process and store much more information than we can on our personal devices.

Diaphragm
A large dome-shaped muscle below the lungs that continually expands and contracts, causing you to breathe in and out.

DNA
The chemical instructions for how a living thing will look and behave. Nearly all living cells contain DNA.

Evolution
The gradual process of change in living things over many generations.

Galaxy
A collection of stars, gas, and dust held together by gravity. Some contain thousands of stars, others trillions.

Habitable zone
The area around a star that is neither too hot nor too cold for living things to survive.

Hypothesis
A prediction or statement that is based on existing knowledge, but not yet tested by experimentation.

Ice age
One of several long periods when the Earth was much colder than it is today and thick sheets of ice covered much of its surface.

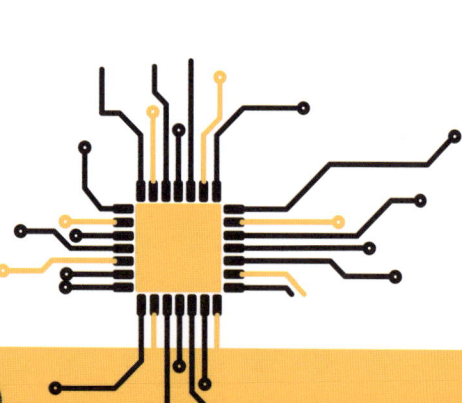

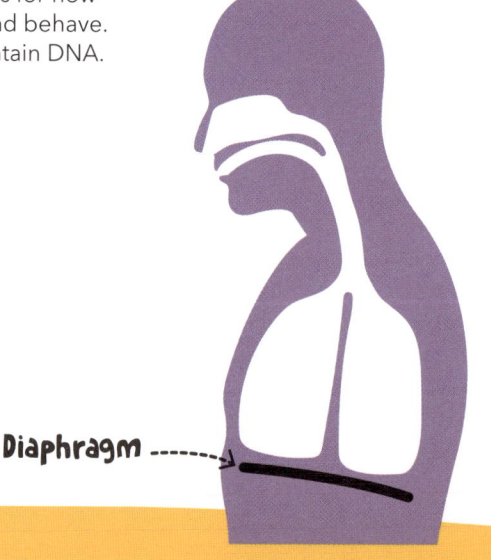

Diaphragm

Immune system
The body's defense system, which protects us from diseases by finding and destroying threats inside the body.

Magnetic field
The force around a magnet that affects nearby objects. Earth has a magnetic field because its outer core acts like a giant magnet.

Mass
A measure of the amount of matter in an object. The more mass an object has, the harder it is to make it start or stop moving, or change the direction it is travelling in.

Matter
The material that everything is made from – anything that has mass and occupies space. Solid, liquid, and gas are states of matter.

Microbe
A tiny organism that we can only see using a microscope. They are also called microorganisms.

Nuclear technology
The process of releasing energy from the centre of atoms. This can then be used to generate power for vehicles or electrical items.

Nucleus
The command center of a cell, containing the DNA that instructs how the cell should look and act. The same word is used for the central core of an atom. Two or more of them are called nuclei.

Orbit
The curved path that one object in space takes around a heavier object, such as a star or planet.

Pollination
The transfer of pollen between plants (or two parts of the same plant), so that reproduction can take place.

Satellite
An object in space that travels around another in orbit. They may be rocks, such as moons, or human-made spacecraft.

Submersible
An underwater vehicle that needs support or power from a larger ship or vessel—unlike a submarine, which can operate independently.

Supercluster
A massive collection of tens of thousands of galaxies grouped together in space.

Tardigrade
Tiny eight-legged microbes also known as "water bears". They can survive extreme conditions that would kill most other forms of life on Earth.

Tube worm
A type of worm that anchors its tail to the seafloor and forms a hard tube around itself for protection.

ACKNOWLEDGMENTS

DK would like to thank:
Jim Green, Stefan Podhorodecki, and Simon Mumford for the cover design; Peter Gee for proofreading; and Elizabeth Wise for the index.

The publisher would like to thank the following for their kind permission to reproduce their photographs:

(Key: a-above; b-below/bottom; c-centre; f-far; l-left; r-right; t-top)

4 Dreamstime.com: VeraOrlova (cl). **10 Alamy Stock Photo:** Brian Hagiwara / Brand X Pictures (cb). **Dreamstime.com:** Dsa144 (bl). **naturepl.com:** Jabruson (tl). **11 Dorling Kindersley:** Natural History Museum, London (bl). **Dreamstime.com:** Isselee (bc); Alexander Potapov (cl); Dinesh Chandra Palrecha (tr). **14 Dreamstime.com:** Mikhail Kokhanchikov / Mik122 (bl); Svetlana Larina / Blair_witch (cl, br); Thawats (crb). **14-15 Dreamstime.com:** VeraOrlova. **15 Dreamstime.com:** Thawats (bc); Svetlana Larina / Blair_witch (tc, cla). **Getty Images / iStock:** GomezDavid (ca). **17 Alamy Stock Photo:** MasPix (tr). **Dorling Kindersley:** Senckenberg Gesellschaft für Naturforschung Museum (c). **18 Alamy Stock Photo:** imageBROKER / F. Schneider (br). **Dreamstime.com:** Andrey Armyagov / Cookelma (cra). **Getty Images / iStock:** John M. Chase (clb). **20 Getty Images:** Picture by Tambako the Jaguar (cra). **21 123RF.com:** Pavlo Vakhrushev / vapi (clb). **23 Dreamstime.com:** Alan Bracken (tr). **Science Photo Library:** A.B. Dowsett (cl). **24 123RF.com:** Ross Taylor (cl); Sebastian Vervenne (tl). **Dreamstime.com:** Xunbin Pan / Defun (bc); Alexander Potapov (bc/fly agaric); Pavel Trankov / Skydie (bc/earthworm); Svetlana Larina / Blair_witch (crb); Georgios Kollidas (cra). **Getty Images / iStock:** Film Studio Aves (cb). **24-25 Getty Images / iStock:** GlobalP (tc). **25 123RF.com:** Tim Hester (c/centipede). **Dreamstime.com:** Richard Griffin (bl); Jaroslav Moravcik (crb); Isselee (c, fbl, tl). **Getty Images / iStock:** kynny (tc, cr). **27 Dreamstime.com:** Galih Wisnu (crb). **28 Getty Images:** Jim Sugar (clb). **29 123RF.com:** 1xpert / Phil Gamble / Dorling Kindersley (crb). **Dreamstime.com:** Wentong Wang (tr). **30 Dreamstime.com:** Santiago Rodríguez Fontoba (bl). **31 Getty Images:** Joel Nito / AFP (cl). **32 Dreamstime.com:** Joseph Khoury (cl). **34 Dreamstime.com:** Antonel (bl). **Getty Images / iStock:** lynnebeclu (cla). **35 Dreamstime.com:** Countrygirl1966 (bl); Svetlana Larina / Blair_witch (cb). **Getty Images / iStock:** Jeff_Hu (crb). **36 Shutterstock.com:** Jason Schronce (cla). **38 ESA / Hubble:** NASA, CXC (clb). **39 Alamy Stock Photo:** Science History Images / Spencer Sutton (cr). **40 NASA:** (bl). **41 Dreamstime.com:** Sebastian Kaulitzki / Eraxion (cr). **ESA:** NASA (cra). **42 NASA:** JPL-Caltech / MSSS (cla). **43 123RF.com:** Leonello Calvetti / Phil Gamble / Dorling Kindersley and Phil Gamble / Dorling Kindersley (cr). **Alamy Stock Photo:** UPI (tr). **NASA:** (cr); Alex Gerst (c). **44 Alamy Stock Photo:** Military Collection (cla). NASA: (cr). **46 NASA:** ESA, CSA, STScI, Brant Robertson (UC Santa Cruz), Ben Johnson (CfA), Sandro Tacchella (Cambridge), Phill Cargile (CfA) (cl x2); ESA / JPL-Caltech (br). **48 Dreamstime.com:** Nerthuz (br). **49 123RF.com:** Leonello Calvetti (tc). **Dreamstime.com:** Koya79 (cr). **50 Science Photo Library:** Lynette Cook (cla). **51 Shutterstock.com:** Jacques Dayan (cra). **52 Dreamstime.com:** Diego Vito Cervo (br). **Getty Images:** Johner Images Royalty-Free / Kari Kohvakka (bc). **55 Dreamstime.com:** Alanjeffery (tr); Pojoslaw (bl). **56 Dreamstime.com:** Iodrakon (cl). **Science Source:** Hank Morgan (cb). **57 Alamy Stock Photo:** Phanie - Sipa Press / BURGER (cr). **59 Getty Images / iStock:** Freder (cra). **60 Dreamstime.com:** Mykola Sosiukin (cla). **61 Getty Images / iStock:** E+ / Imgorthand (cra). **62 Dreamstime.com:** Alexander Shalamov (clb). **63 Alamy Stock Photo:** Connect Images / Andrew Brookes (tc). **64 Dreamstime.com:** Starast (cr). **65 Dreamstime.com:** Mark Higgins / Markrhiggins (tr). **66 Dreamstime.com:** MaxiSports (b). **Getty Images:** Hulton Archive / Stringer (cla). **67 Dreamstime.com:** Soloway (br). **Getty Images / iStock:** antoniokhr (tc). **68 Dreamstime.com:** David Fowler (cr). **69 Adobe Stock:** zombiu26 (r). **71 NASA:** (tc). **72 Alamy Stock Photo:** Science History Images / Photo Researchers (cla). **Shutterstock.com:** Gorodenkoff (c). **73 Dreamstime.com:** Kts (cra). **74 Getty Images / iStock:** DieterMeyrl (bl). **75 Alamy Stock Photo:** Associated Press / Jae C. Hong (cl)

Cover images: Front: 123RF.com: Pavlo Vakhrushev / vapi (jellyfish); **Adobe Stock:** Khai (mammoth); **Dreamstime.com:** Alle (bc), Alexander Potapov (tr), Soleilc (cb / mountains), Svetlana Larina / Blair_witch (butterfly)

INDEX

Main topics are shown in **bold** page numbers.

A
acceleration 44
aging **52-53**
air pressure 68, 69
airplanes 44, **68-69**
aliens **40-41**
Andromeda 46
Apollo 10 44
appendix **64-65**
artificial intelligence (AI) 73, **74-75**
asteroids 11, 50

B
bacteria 23, 27, 65
balance 67, 68
bats 21
bees 34, 37
beetles **10-11**
bicycles **66-67**
Big Bang 38-39
birds 14, 25, 35
braille 63
brain 20-21, 56-57, 74
butterflies **14-15**

C
cells 23, 52, 65
Challenger Deep 26
chimpanzees 54, 55, 63
chips 72, 73
claws 19, 27
communication 32-33, 54, 59
computers **72-73**, **74-75**
crabs **18-19**, 27
crustaceans 18
cycads 34

D
dark energy 38
data centers 72, 73
diaphragm 60, 61
digestive system 20, 64
dinosaurs 16-17
DNA 53
dodos 25
dogs 25
dolphins 21
dreams **56-57**

E
Earth 22-23, 28-29, 43, 71
  and gravity 48-49
  and the moon 50-51
earthquakes 27, **30-31**
elephants 12, 17, 20
emotions 54-55, 56-57
Enceladus 41
endorphins 55
engines 44, 68
evolution 18-19, 21, 34, 65
exoplanets 40-41
experiments 8-9
extinction 11, **12-13**, 17, 25

F
false crabs 18
fault lines 30
fingerprints **62-63**
fish 26, 27
flowers 10, **34-35**, 36-37
fossils 11, 17
fungi 33

G
galaxies 29, 38, 46
giraffes 20
grass 32
gravity 39, **48-49**, 50-51, 71
grooming 55
gyroscopic effect 66

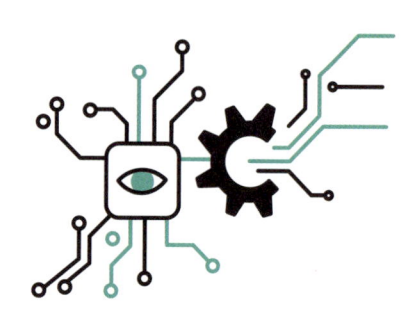

H
habitable zones 41
Hawking, Stephen 70
hiccups **60-61**
humanoid robot 75
humans 13, 21, **44-45**, 65
  see also artificial intelligence (AI)
hydrogen 28, 29

I
immune system 65
infections 13, 65
insects 10-11, 14-15
International Space Station (ISS) 45, 71
intestines 64

JK
James Webb Space Telescope 47
jellyfish 21
Jupiter 40, 48
koalas 62, 65

L
ladybugs 11
laughter **54-55**
leopards 62
life on Earth **22-23**
lifespans 53
lift 68, 69
lightning 22
light-years 46-47
Linnaeus, Carl 24
lizards 25
lobsters 18
lungs 20, 55, 60

M

magnetic fields 14, 31
mammoths **12-13**
Mars 40, 42, 43, 45
medicines 55
memories 21, 56-57
memory chips 72
microbes 13, 41
microprocessors 73
migration **14-15**
mobile phones 73
monarch butterflies 14-15
moons 40, 41
   Earth's moon 42, 44, **50-51**
muscles 20, 55, 58

N

nectar 11, 34
nerves 21, 61, 63
Newton, Isaac 7, 48
nightmares 57
nuclear technology 44
nucleus 52

O

oceans **26-27**, 29, 40
orangutans 54
orbits 45, 49
oxygen 29, 42, 58

P

photons 45, 49
pincers 19
planets 40-41, **42-43**, 48, 50
   see also Earth
plants **32-33**
flowers 10, **34-35**, 36-37
plates **16-17**
pollination 11, 34-35, 37
predators 19, 32
pressure, air 68, 69
pressure, water 26, 27

Q

quantum computing 73

R

reproduction, plant 34-35
roots 33

S

satellites 40, 49, 71
Saturn 40
seafloor 22, 26
single-cell organisms 23
sleep **20-21**, 56-57
smart phones 73
social behavior 17, 54, 59
solar system 28, 40, 50
spacecraft 40, 43, 44
space-time 70, 71
species 10-11, 19, **24-25**, 34
speed **44-45**, 71
squid 27
Stegosaurus **16-17**
stomach 61, 64
stromatolites 23
submersibles 26
sun 14, 35, 36-37, 42
sunflowers **36-37**

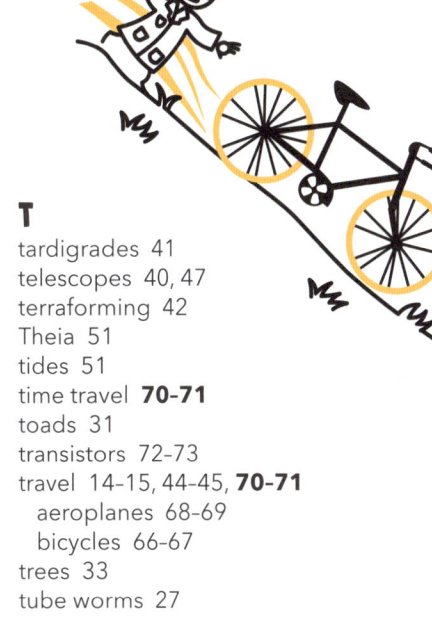

T

tardigrades 41
telescopes 40, 47
terraforming 42
Theia 51
tides 51
time travel **70-71**
toads 31
transistors 72-73
travel 14-15, 44-45, **70-71**
   aeroplanes 68-69
   bicycles 66-67
trees 33
tube worms 27

U

universe **38-39**, 41, **46-47**, 49

V

velocity 49
Venus 40
volcanoes 22-23, 28, 31

W

warp drive 45
water 22, **28-29**, 41
whales 21, 27
wheels 66-67
wings, airplane 68-69
woolly mammoths **12-13**
wormholes 45

Y

yawning **58-59**

About the ROYAL INSTITUTION

The Royal Institution (Ri) is an independent science charity based in London, England. It was founded in 1799 with a clear vision: to be a place where anyone could come to enjoy learning about science, and the world around us. Many amazing people have worked here over the last 200-plus years. In fact, scientists who worked at the Ri have discovered 10 elements of the periodic table, and won an amazing 15 Nobel prizes!

Today we spend our time running exciting activities for people of all ages to discover the wonders of science. Maybe you have seen our Christmas Lectures—science lectures for young people just like you—which are broadcast on the UK's BBC every year. We also run stuff throughout the year, from explosion-packed talks to interactive science workshops. We also travel to schools all across the UK. Here at the Ri, we believe that science is for everyone, especially you!

Find out more at **rigb.org** and **youtube.com/theroyalinstitution**

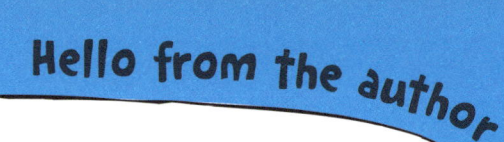

Hello from the author

Hi there, I'm Peter, and I really hope you enjoyed reading this book! Since being a child, I have always loved learning about science and exploring nature, whether it was reading my animal atlas or simply exploring in the woods. As an adult, I continued with this passion. First, I studied Zoology at the University of Sheffield in England, before living in the Alps in Switzerland, showing young people the amazing nature and wildlife there. I am excited now to be working with the Royal Institution, writing exciting books like this one!